Introduction

Briefly, the authors' objective has been to provide a pictorial history of those scout/fighter aircraft that served in an operational capacity with the RAF from January 1920 until the last day of 1939 – a period in which Britain once again moved from an era of peace to war with an old enemy, albeit this time the enemy would be Hitler's totalitarian National Socialist Germany as opposed to the Imperial Germany of old.

As well as illustrating each of the fighter types used during the inter-war period with as many of their squadrons and units as we could muster, the images themselves will, it is hoped, also convey a sense of the technical advances that rapidly took root within Britain's aero industries from the mid-1930s onwards.

Martin Derry & Neil Robinson

Unless otherwise stated all photos are provided by or via the authors.

Acknowledgements

The authors would very much like to thank the following for their help and generous assistance in providing many of the images contained within this work, namely: Tony Buttler, Tony O'Toole and Carl Vincent. In addition, we wish to firmly acknowledge our gratitude to Tom Ketley who allowed us to access his late father's extensive photo archive of pre-war aircraft, as well as Martin Mace from Pen & Sword for his ongoing support and encouragement.

Of course, we are as ever truly grateful to Mark Gauntlet for his superb colour illustrations, given that here, instead of there being just one or two aircraft to cover, there are no less than fourteen basic airframes in this volume. Seriously, many thanks again Mark, perhaps you can prepare yourself for Part Two – the bombers!

Left:
On 31 August 1918 the RAF had 562 F.E.2bs and F.E.2cs on charge, a remarkable quantity given that the basic airframe had entered service in 1914. By 1917 the type was, by Western Front standards, obsolete and terribly vulnerable for use in daylight operations but remained useful as a night bomber and with the Home Defence fighter units in Britain, some of which were modified as single-seat fighters. In its own way this image helps define aviation during the Great War era, it wasn't all about the famous Camel and S.E.5A. Seen here is an ex-RFC/RAF F.E.2b which survived long enough to be sold into civilian use albeit while still retaining its original military serial and underwing roundels. D3832 became the only F.E.2b to enter the civilian market and later received the civil registration G-EAHC in August 1919: it was withdrawn from use (WFU) on 7 August 1921.

Below:
The highly regarded multi-purpose two-seat Bristol F.2B Fighter would continue to serve the RAF into the 1930s albeit no longer as a scout (fighter) beyond 1919/early 1920. This anonymous example, coded 'C', was photographed when serving on the Western Front in 1918, with the presence of air and groundcrew lending scale to the F.2B's size. The gunner's Lewis gun is pointing skywards; often two such weapons were carried in the rear cockpit.

Top:
The appealing lines of Sopwith Snipe E6965 is seen in flight while serving with 1 Squadron in Iraq c.1922/23 with Vickers Vernon I transports in the background. Vernons entered RAF service in 1922 with the first examples going to 45 Squadron which moved to Hinaidi, Iraq, in April 1922. By April 1924, Snipe E6965 was back in the UK where it served briefly with 41 Squadron prior to joining 19 Squadron. Thereafter E6965 was allocated to a meteorological flight in mid-1925 although its ultimate fate is uncertain. As the post-war need to camouflage aircraft diminished a superior cellulose-based dope, V84 'Aluminium', was gradually introduced on new airframes or when older WWI aircraft, such as E6965, were re-doped.

Bottom:
Lacking any further detail, we know only that Snipe E7514 served with 1 Squadron in Iraq which, judging by the clothing and headgear on display seems likely. Interestingly, rather than overall Aluminium, this Snipe is finished in either WW1-type PC10 or, more likely, the reddish-brown shade known as PC12 which was more resistant to the penetration of the sun's rays. Less vulnerable to the sun, the under surfaces would have been finished in a transparent clear dope, often referred to as Clear Doped Linen, through which the natural light creamy-fawn colour of linen showed. For clarity, the wing and fuselage roundels are outlined with a white inch-wide surround. At this time, and for years to come, rudder striping would continue to be applied with blue forward i.e., blue nearest the rudder post.

The Roaring 1920s

When World War I ended the recently established Royal Air Force was, unsurprisingly, awash with aircraft of all descriptions; more surprising perhaps was the fact that despite an ongoing cull of obsolescing types, on the last day of *1919* the RAF still possessed 9,122 non-obsolete aircraft (with 1,100 more assigned to the Fleet Air Arm). Whilst the famous S.E.5A and Sopwith Camel had by this time been largely (yet not entirely) consigned to history, the RAF possessed no less than 1,860 Sopwith Snipes which, from 1920, would become the RAF's standard single-seat fighter for years to come.

Other core types on charge on 31 December 1919 included approximately 1,650 Bristol F.2B Fighters and 1,250 De Havilland DH.9As which, together with the Snipe, accounted for over fifty per cent of the RAF's inventory at that time with Avro 504 training aircraft accounting for a further 2,700 airframes.

Further notable types initially stored for possible future use by the RAF included: 108 Vickers Vimy bombers, 265 Handley Page O/400s, approximately 52 V/1500 bombers, 186 DH.10 bombers and around 270 Martinsyde F.4 Buzzard fighters. (While a few of the latter – capable of 145 mph at sea level – were issued to the RAF following the Armistice the Buzzard, which enjoyed a much superior performance to the Snipe, was never adopted as a fighter.)

Sopwith Snipe
In the post-war period Snipes eventually served with twelve RAF squadrons during

the 1920s and became the RAF's last rotary-engined fighter. Regrettably, in 1920, hundreds of brand-new Snipes were summarily disposed of so rapidly that a programme had to be quickly implemented in 1921 to ensure that damaged Snipes would be repaired rather than automatically scrapped. Ultimately over 200 were thus spared and returned to service, enabling squadron complements to be maintained – just!

Gloster Grebe II

The RAF's second fighter of the 1920s was the single-seat Gloucestershire * Grebe II (the Grebe I didn't enter series production) of which 109† were procured, plus twenty Grebe IIIDC two-seaters. Powered by an Armstrong Siddeley Jaguar IV radial engine the Grebe II achieved 161 mph at sea level, approximately 36 mph more than the Snipe, both of which carried the same WWI armament of two fixed .303in Vickers machine guns – a near-standard armament that would be applied to all RAF biplane fighters prior to the arrival of the Gloster Gladiator.

* In December 1926, the decision was made to simplify the Gloucestershire Aircraft Co Ltd.'s name to 'Gloster'. For simplicity's sake the latter is used throughout.

† One of which, J7585, was delivered as, or was soon converted to DC configuration.

Armstrong Whitworth Siskin III

Made distinctive by its V-shaped interplane struts and sesquiplane wing design, the Armstrong Whitworth Siskin III single-seat fighter first entered RAF service in May 1924 with 41 Squadron, followed by 111 Squadron a few weeks later. Siskin production totals have become blurred over the years with more than a hint of confusion being created by the production of the Siskin III, III(DC) and IIIA; the whole becoming further muddied by the later conversion of thirty-plus single-seat Siskin IIIs into two-seat III(DC)s.

However, if prototype J6583 is ignored, it appears that fifty-six Siskin IIIs were procured with most going to the RAF. Of

Continued on page 7

Top:
Snipes from 1 Squadron with the nearest, F2457, missing its fuselage roundel and both wheel hub covers. F2457 served with the unit from May 1923 to October 1924, beyond which further details are missing. E7642 (second in line) was delivered to the Iraq Aircraft Depot, Hinaidi, in September 1923 for issue to 1 Squadron. Later returned to the UK, E7642 was with the Home Aircraft Depot (HAD) at Henlow by April 1927 presumably awaiting final disposal.

Bottom:
Seen in 1925, Snipe E7561 served with 1 School of Technical Training (SoTT) for two years from September 1924. The last operational Snipes were withdrawn in November 1926, although a few served for a little longer in secondary roles with odd examples being allocated to 1 and 5 Flying Training Schools (FTS) as late as January 1928. Additionally, at least three dual-control airframes, the Snipe(DC), served well into 1928 and it appears that the RAF's last flyable Snipe was probably Snipe(DC), E6478, which was apparently issued to 17 Squadron in July or August 1928, its ultimate fate being unrecorded. When photographed, E7561 was in immaculate condition with all the correct markings for the period including 25 inch diameter red/white/blue fuselage roundels and 8 inch high serial numbers on the fuselage and rudder in typical Sopwith style. For the record, its upper and lower mainplane roundels (the latter just discernible) were 56 inches in diameter.

Centre:
An undated image of Gloster Grebe II, J7363, seen while serving with 25 Squadron from December 1925 to May 1927. However, J7402 (behind) joined the unit in October 1926 thus reducing the time frame somewhat. Grebes were amongst the first post-war RAF aircraft to feature squadron markings and here the aircraft all display the unit's modified (broader) black parallel bars on the forward fuselage as well as between the roundels on the upper wing. J7363 differs slightly in that it was the mount of S/Ldr A H Peck, the commanding officer (CO) and is made more easily identifiable by virtue of the black band aft of the fuselage roundel, another around both surfaces of the lower wings, plus black wheel hubs. Grebes were used by 25 Squadron until July 1929, thereafter J7402 seems to have been stored until 1930 when it was issued to the Armament and Gunnery School (A&GS) and A&AEE.

Bottom:
From September 1925 to August 1926 Grebe II J7381 served with 29 Squadron whose distinctive fuselage markings, consisting of four red 'X's flanked by red bars are evident here. Four further red 'X's flanked by red bars adorned the upper mainplane between the roundels. Sold to New Zealand in March 1928 as NZ501 (later becoming A-5) it served until November 1938. Two further examples, J7394 and J7400, were also supplied to New Zealand. The Grebe's 'S.E.5-style' fin and rudder are clearly evident.

Left:
Grebe II J7288 seen in flight during the period October 1924 to April 1926, after which this airframe's history disappears from the record. J7288 was part of the first production batch of twelve aircraft, ten of which including J7288 went to 25 Squadron commencing October 1924. The unit's parallel black fuselage bars are narrower than those seen on J7363 (below) but in this case they continue forward onto the exhaust collector ring.

Top:
Seen wearing 32 Squadron's interrupted broad blue bar along the length of its fuselage (repeated on top of the upper mainplane) is Grebe II, J7571, which served with this unit in early 1927 prior to joining 29 Squadron in June. Thereafter the record is unclear except to say that it was rebuilt as JR7571 at Hinaidi, Iraq, c.1928/29 prior to being allocated to 4 FTS at Abu Sueir, Egypt, in 1930 where pilot training was undertaken far removed from the poor weather conditions experienced at home. JR7571 appears to have survived until February 1931.

Centre:
Three unidentified Grebes pose at an unknown location on an unknown date, their identities being either unreadable or bodily obscured by the 32 Squadron machine nearest the camera: the Grebe on the left carries 29 Squadron markings. There is a suggestion that this trio could be J7367, J7397 and J7402, i.e. the trio operated by the A&AEE in 1930, the suggestion, however, remains speculative at best.

Bottom:
When 19 Squadron replaced its Snipes with Grebes in December 1924, they originally selected unit markings that were quite different from the more familiar alternating blue and white checks adopted later during the Grebe's service. Seen here in their original form, an unidentified 19 Squadron Grebe displays the pattern as it originally existed, namely two blue parallel lines on the fuselage with broader blue diagonals separating them and extending as far aft as the roundel. Presumably the design was repeated on the upper wing, although it is not certain.

Top:
Twenty Grebe IIIDC two-seat trainers were ordered for the RAF of which J7525 was one. Initially allocated to 19 Squadron in July 1925, it is thought that this photo was taken at Leuchars, Fife, where J7525 is known to have been based from February 1926 to March 1928. Devoid of any unit markings, this Grebe appears to have 'dark' forward fuselage panelling which, as with the wheel hub covers, could have been red. A handful of Grebe IIIDCs continued to serve into 1931, known examples being J7536 with the A&GS, J7537 with 5 FTS and J7585 (the converted Grebe II) which was allocated to Hendon in January 1931. As for single-seaters, J7383 was still serving with 3 FTS in June 1931, but whether or not it outlived the A&AEE trio (see table) remains unclear.

Centre:
This less than flattering image of Grebe IIIDC, J7535, is included to show that at least some two-seat trainers did carry squadron markings as well as single-seaters; in this case 56 Squadron's red and white checks which would likely have been repeated on its now inverted upper wing. J7535 joined the unit in February 1926, surviving only until August when it overturned on landing. One wonders if this image relates to an earlier incident as, on the face of it at least, the damage appears to be minimal.

Above:
The initial production order for the Siskin III amounted to three hand-built airframes: J6981-J6983. J6982, seen here, was probably photographed when attached to the Aeroplane Experimental Establishment in 1923 (redesignated as the A&AEE on 24 March 1924), or with the Royal Aircraft Establishment (RAE) Farnborough, in 1924. Temporarily registered as G-EBJS for the 1924 King's Cup Air Race, J6982 was finally delivered to the RAF in November 1924. Worthy of comment are the 1-2-3 ratio roundel dimensions with the large red centre, a feature of Armstrong Whitworth-built aeroplanes, while the fuselage serial lacks a hyphen between the letter and the numbers which was quite unusual for aircraft of this period.

Top:
Siskin III, J7764, seen while serving with 41 Squadron in 1926. After serving with Duxford's meteorological flight in 1927 it was returned to the makers for conversion to a IIIDC and thereafter served with 3 FTS then 5 FTS from May 1929 to October 1931. As with all RAF fighters of the period, Siskins carried twin Vickers machine guns that were subject to frequent stoppages, however, a positive of sorts emerged inasmuch that whereas it was a manoeuvrable aircraft it was also stable at 'ordinary' flying speeds, thus allowing a mallet-wielding pilot the opportunity to clear a stoppage during those moments when the Siskin 'was looking after itself'. J7764 displays 41 Squadron's broad red bar ahead of the fuselage roundel which was later extended along the fuselage (flanking the roundel) to terminate just beneath the leading edge of the tailplane. Similarly, a red bar was applied to the upper mainplane between the roundels. The aircraft behind J7764 is a Snipe, 41 Squadron having relinquished the type two years earlier.

Continued from page 3

that figure, one was retained by the manufacturer until it crashed in late 1923; at least two were used by the A&AEE and never issued to an RAF squadron; two others, J7758 and J7759, were allocated to the RCAF (Royal Canadian Air Force) in December 1925 and at least three more were converted to DC pattern prior to delivery, leaving perhaps forty-eight examples to be issued to 41 and 111 Squadrons. Ultimately the Siskin IIIDC became the most numerous variant of the original design as fifty-three were ordered from new, their numbers swollen by the conversion of surviving Mk.IIIs to Mk.III(DC) as they became surplus to requirements, while at least two Mk.IIIs were converted to Siskin IIIA standard. Powered by a 325hp Armstrong Siddeley Jaguar III 14-cylinder radial engine, the Siskin III could achieve 134 mph at sea level.

Hawker Woodcock II
The single-seat Hawker Woodcock II first entered RAF service in May 1925. Although production ran to sixty-three airframes confusion may occasionally arise given that serial numbers J7592-J7595 – already applied to Grebes – were mistakenly applied to four Woodcocks in lieu of their correct serials J8313-J8316, temporarily resulting in a spurious total of sixty-seven airframes (plus two prototypes). Powered by a 425hp Bristol Jupiter IV 9-cylinder radial engine, the Woodcock II achieved almost 141 mph at sea level, offering little extra in performance over the Siskin or Snipe.

Due to its wide track undercarriage and the positioning of its guns, which apparently hid the weapons' muzzle flash from the pilot, the Woodcock was later deemed suitable as a night fighter, consequently, both 3 and 17 Squadrons were duly tasked with night defence

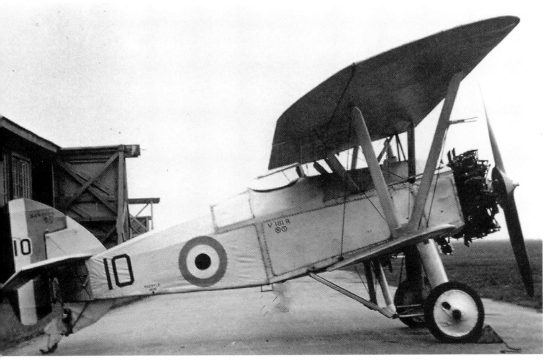

Bottom:
This excellent image illustrates the starboard side of a Siskin III, in this instance an RCAF example, serial number 10, (previously RAF serial J7759). Sent to Canada in late 1925, it joined 2 Squadron RCAF (founded on 1 April 1924) in June 1926. Later serialed 301, it crashed in October 1934 and was SOC in March 1935. Photo supplied by **Carl Vincent**

Top:
Ordered as a Siskin IIIDC and first flown in July 1928, J9198 was allocated to 54 Squadron in 1930 along with several others. Re-formed as a fighter unit in January 1930, 54 Squadron flew the IIIDC throughout 1930, its promised Bulldogs being delivered between April and October. Finished in Aluminium overall it is devoid of squadron markings, in fact it would seem that none of their IIIDCs ever received the unit's distinctive but short-lived yellow bars that were generally applied to the fuselage and upper wing. J9198 went on to serve with 111 and 25 Squadrons before joining 5 FTS in September 1933.

Bottom:
Hawker Woodcock II, J7960, served with 17 Squadron from December 1926 to 1928 and clearly displays the unit's black parallel zig-zag bars which, in this instance at least, extend the length of the fuselage to terminate aft of the serial number; on others they terminated short of the serial number. The black zig-zag markings were repeated on all 17 Squadron Woodcocks along the full span of the upper mainplane between the roundels, while their forward fuselage panels were painted in a dark grey that contrasted sharply with the overall Aluminium dope finish. Although hard to distinguish, the port machine gun can just be seen mounted on brackets outside and below the cockpit coaming and thus accessible to the pilot when clearing a jam. Woodcocks were rapidly disposed of following withdrawal in 1928, the last service example is believed to have been J8303 which remained with Halton's station flight into 1929, its final fate seemingly unrecorded.

duties until, on 21 August 1928, the type was grounded following a series of accidents caused by structural weaknesses although by that time 17 Squadron had relinquished its Woodcocks several months earlier.

Gloster Gamecock I
The RAF's last wooden biplane fighter, the Gamecock I looked similar to the Grebe with the primary difference focusing on the engine – the Grebe's Jaguar IV having been replaced by a radial 425hp Bristol Jupiter VI or VII enabling the Gamecock to achieve a maximum of 154 mph at sea level. A less obvious change centred on the Gamecock's twin Vickers guns which were mounted in the lower forward fuselage with their breech blocks placed inside the cockpit on either side of the pilot's seat, the barrels were sited in recessed external troughs with rounds exiting between pairs of cylinders: the latter made possible because of the 9-cylinder layout of its Jupiter but impossible with the Grebe's 14-cylinder Jaguar.

Three prototypes preceded ninety production Gamecock Is, the latter entering squadron service in April 1926 with 23 and 43 Squadrons followed by three more squadrons at later dates. Most left operational service in 1928 and 1929 with only 23 Squadron retaining the type into the 1930s.

Although a company-sponsored project led to Mk.I, J7910, being converted to Mk.II standard it was ultimately rejected by the RAF, despite which, fifteen Gamecock IIs (plus two pattern aircraft) were bought by the Finnish Air Force in 1928 and were still in service as fighter trainers at the start of the 1939 Winter War, the last not being retired until 1944.

Bristol F.2B Fighter
The two-seat Bristol F.2B Fighter continued to serve the post-war RAF for many years. However, despite its name,

the Bristol Fighter is excluded from this volume given that its role as a fighter per se altered in 1919/20 as its performance began to lag by comparison with later fighter aircraft. Nevertheless, the F.2B would prove itself to be of great value in other roles, namely as a reconnaissance, army co-operation and dual-control training aircraft at home and abroad. Both the F.2B (and D.H.9A) will appear in a subsequent volume.

Nieuport and General Aircraft Company Nighthawk and Nightjar

Occasionally and erroneously referred to as an operational fighter, the Nighthawk is included to amplify the fact that only a small batch was obtained by the RAF, of which two or three were attached to 1 Squadron in Mesopotamia between April and September 1923 for service trials. Of greater importance was its legacy. Largely designed by H P Folland, creator of the S.E.5 series of fighters for the RFC, the Nighthawk was the RAF's first post-war fighter to be fitted with a radial (as opposed to rotary) engine and as such set a pattern for RAF single-seat fighters prior to the arrival of the multi-gun Gloster Gladiator (Hawker Furies excepted).

Related to the Nighthawk, the **Nightjar** was a rotary-engined deck-landing fighter of which approximately twenty were acquired by the RAF, some being issued to 203 Squadron in 1922 to replace its ageing Camels.

Above:
Gloster Gamecock J7757 captures the external differences that distinguished it from the Grebe. Obvious features such as the rudder and engine are clearly evident, while the low-mounted gun troughs are less so. The third of three prototypes, this airframe was tested by the A&AEE and RAE from September 1925 until 19 December 1927 when it made its last flight. Although much of the airframe is finished in Aluminium, areas of dark grey panelling around the engine and cockpit coaming are evident with the area to the rear of the cockpit probably finished in pale grey. J7757's markings were standard for the period with roundels still being applied in VR3 Bright Red and VB2 Bright Blue shades. Usually, fuselage roundels were 25 inches in diameter, but in the Gamecock's case, because its fuselage was so short, 20 inch diameter roundels were substituted; even then, the placing of the serial using 8 inch high characters with a hyphen was a tight fit. Gamecock upper and lower mainplane roundels were set at 56 inches in diameter, a size determined by the aircraft's wing chord, essentially spanning it from leading to trailing edge.

Top:
Woodcock II, J8292 leads J8303 and one other 3 Squadron machine into the air at Upavon, Wiltshire, the unit's home airfield since April 1924 and where it would be joined by 17 Squadron in October 1926. Although this photo is undated, J8292 joined the unit in March 1927 and was SOC following an accident with a Siskin in July 1928. J8303 was allocated to 3 Squadron in October 1927, so for that reason this image must date from between late 1927 and July 1928, shortly before Woodcocks were removed from squadron use. The squadron adopted an emerald green stripe which was applied to the length of the fuselage, interrupted only by the roundel and serial number, the stripe was also applied along the span of the upper mainplane from roundel to roundel.

Top:
Gamecock J7920 joined 43 Squadron in April 1926 and remained with the unit into the following year, thereafter the record is vague, but it is known that J7920 was being used by the Home Aircraft Depot Station Flight at Henlow from August 1928 to March 1929. As related previously with Gamecock J7757, the type's short fuselage meant that the placing of squadron markings had to be purposefully considered thus 43 Squadron's black and white fuselage checks extended only from the engine bay to the roundel. As can be seen, the unit's black and white checks were also applied to the upper mainplane.

Centre:
An interesting photo inasmuch that J8033 clearly reveals its additional V-shaped struts that were added to some Gamecocks (but not all) in 1927 in an attempt to cure the dreaded phenomenon of wing flutter (failure) that plagued both the Gamecock and the earlier Grebe. Other wing stiffening measures were also tried and it seems that they ultimately proved successful enough to allow the V-struts to be later removed. J8033 is known to have served with the A&GS from April 1928 to October 1930.

Above:
Gamecock J8074 belonged to 23 Squadron and was photographed between April 1928, when it left 32 Squadron, and June 1929 when it joined 3 Squadron following which it served with the Central Flying School (CFS) until it crashed in Kent on 22 October 1930. Scarcely visible just aft of the horizontal engine cylinder is J8074's individual code letter 'G', while 23 Squadron's motif, an eagle preying on a falcon, is readily apparent on the fin. Apart from the fuselage panelling around the engine and cockpit area, which was either grey or dark green, this image also shows the unit's red and blue bars running along the fuselage from engine bay to empennage, inside the gun trough, and spanwise on the upper mainplane between the roundels.

Left:
A line up of 23 Squadron Gloster Gamecock Is at RAF Henlow c.1930. Notice that the rudder stripe colours are now reversed with red leading followed by white and blue, the result of a change introduced by the Air Ministry in 1930. This image offers another view of the unit's red and blue bars on the fuselage if not quite the upper mainplane. It is believed that the nearest aircraft, J8084, belonged to the CO, S/Ldr Raymond Collishaw (the famous WWI leader of 'Black Flight' 10 Naval Air Squadron), as it has a squadron leader's pennant under the cockpit. J8084 was struck by a taxiing Bulldog on 31 March 1931 and presumably SOC as a result.

TABLE of RAF SINGLE-SEAT FIGHTER SQUADRONS 1920 TO 1929

Snipe-equipped squadrons 1920 to 1926
1 Sqn – To India 1.20. Snipes received 2.20. To Iraq 1.4.20. Snipes in use to 11.26 (last operational Snipe squadron)
3 Sqn – 6.20 to 3.21 (Based in India). Re-formed UK 4.24. Snipes used 4.24 to 8.25
17 Sqn – Re-formed UK 4.24. Snipes used 4.24 to 3.26
19 Sqn – Re-formed UK 4.23. Snipes used 4.23 to 12.24
23 Sqn – Re-formed UK 7.25. Snipes used 7.25 to 4.26
25 Sqn – Re-formed UK 4.20. Snipes used 4.20 to 10.24 (To Turkey 9.22 re Chanak Crisis. UK by 10.23)
29 Sqn – Re-formed UK 4.23. Snipes used 4.23 to 1.25
32 Sqn – Re-formed UK 4.23. Snipes used 4.23 to 12.24
41 Sqn – Re-formed UK 4.23. Snipes used 4.23 to 5.24
43 Sqn – Re-formed UK 7.25. Snipes used 7.25 to 5.26
56 Sqn – Re-formed Egypt 2.20. Snipes used until 9.22 when disbanded. Re-formed UK 11.22. Snipes used to 11.24
111 Sqn – Re-formed UK 10.23 with Grebes (single flight). Snipes served 4.24 to 1.25

Grebe II - equipped squadrons 1923 to 1929
19 Sqn – Grebe II used 12.24 to 4.28
25 Sqn – Grebe II used 10.24 to 6.29
29 Sqn – Grebe II used 1.25 to 3.28
32 Sqn – Grebe II used 11.24 to 2.27
56 Sqn – Grebe II used 9.24 to 9.27
111 Sqn – Grebe II used 10.23 to 1.25 (single flight of six Grebes – but see 'Snipe 111 Sqn')
Note: 15 and or 22 Squadron notionally operated three Grebes (plus other types) under the auspices of the A&AEE. Reportedly, the trio made the type's last public appearance at an air display in 1931.

Siskin III-equipped squadrons 1924 to 1927
41 Sqn – Siskin III used 5.24 to 4.27
111 Sqn – Siskin III used 6.24 to 11.26

Woodcock II-equipped squadrons 1925 to 1928
3 Sqn – Woodcocks used 5.25 to 8.28
17 Sqn – Woodcocks used 3.26 to 1.28

Gamecock-equipped squadrons 1926 to 1931
3 Sqn – Gamecocks used 8.28 to 7.29
17 Sqn – Gamecocks used 1.28 to 9.28
23 Sqn – Gamecocks used 4.26 to 9.31
32 Sqn – Gamecocks used 9.26 to 4.28
43 Sqn – Gamecocks used 4.26 to 6.28

NOTE:
Many readers will be aware that the Armstrong Whitworth **Siskin IIIA** and Bristol **Bulldog** entered squadron service during the later 1920s. For convenience, given that both remained in operational service well beyond January 1930, they are included in **Appendix 1: Fighter Squadrons and their aircraft 1930 to December 1939.**

The path to conflict

Following the German invasion of Poland on 1 September 1939, Britain and France declared war against Germany two days later – a year after the Munich crisis of late September 1938. In retrospect it is useful to regard that crisis as a 'wake-up' call to the British people, despite Neville Chamberlain's speech following his return from Munich in which he advised '...I believe it is peace for our time.' In reality war was already inevitable.

Chamberlain was referring to an agreement whereby British, French, Italian and German leaders (Chamberlain, Daladier, Mussolini, and Hitler respectively) had arrived at a political 'understanding' in which the Sudetenland, a fortified region of Czechoslovakia, was to be ceded to Nazi Germany. This agreement, reached in conference on 29 September 1938 and termed the Munich Agreement, was achieved without Czech government representatives being present: their request to attend having been refused by Hitler.

Chamberlain was a committed supporter of appeasement toward Hitler, a policy both he and Daladier believed necessary to avert a European war and ensure a lasting peace. Did Chamberlain honestly believe he had indeed brokered a lasting peace? Probably, initially, but when in March 1939 Hitler annexed the remaining Czech lands of Bohemia and Moravia, and Slovakia became a German puppet state, even Chamberlain accepted that war was inevitable.

Importantly and despite the political rhetoric, Chamberlain's '...peace for our time' did buy actual time, eleven months as it turned out, a period that allowed Britain's armed forces to further accelerate its preparations for war. Why 'further accelerate'? Because the need to improve and expand Britain's armed forces didn't commence as a result of Czechoslovakia's dismemberment – it had commenced as long ago as 1934.

Munich was one in a long sequence of events leading inexorably to war, a war which Winston Churchill always believed was simply a continuation of World War I. That Germany had been ruined financially and politically by the Great War is undeniable, but because much of the country was left unoccupied by Allied forces it remained undefeated in the eyes of most Germans. The terms of the 1919 Versailles Treaty caused great bitterness among the populace which quickly allowed extremist political parties to flourish and survive in a republic largely devoid of a stable political system. During the 1920s several extreme political factions grew, destabilizing then eradicating whatever remained of a balanced political system. Ultimately, only the most ruthless succeeded and it scarcely needs recording that the most ruthless of them all was the Nazi Party under Adolf Hitler.

From the outset, Hitler strove to increase the power of all arms of the German military with increasingly large rearmament programmes in contravention of the 1925 Treaty of Locarno which in turn emphasized, in Germany's case, the restrictions imposed at Versailles concerning the size of the land and sea forces permitted to them and prohibited a German military air force. The Locarno Treaty also outlawed any acts of aggression between the signatories, of which Germany was one. Hitler's new measures went hand-in-hand with his avowed intent to incorporate all of Europe's Teutonic peoples into a Greater Germany.

In March 1935 Hitler repudiated the Versailles Treaty: Britain and France, lacking both will and determination, did nothing. In 1936, Hitler's forces entered and re-militarized the Rhineland, a buffer

Below:
By the beginning of the 1930s RAF single-seat biplane fighters hadn't advanced very much since World War I. They retained, like the Nighthawk a decade earlier, fabric-covered wings and rear fuselage, an open cockpit, fixed undercarriage and two fixed machine guns. This anonymous Hawker Fury I belongs to 43 Squadron which operated the type from May 1931 to January 1939.

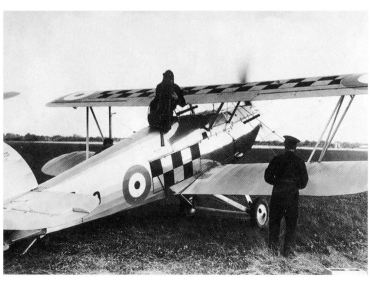

zone between Germany and France established after WWI, and again not a finger was lifted against him beyond limp diplomatic protests. Emboldened, Austria, a country rich with iron-ore deposits, was taken into Hitler's orbit in March 1938, following which, as related, he demanded and received the Czech Sudetenland later in 1938, annexed the rest of the country in March 1939, the Lithuanian port of Memel in the same month, and culminated in invading Poland on 1 September 1939. He ignored all protestations from other nations and, specifically, warnings from Britain and France that his actions would lead to war.

Although the three volumes of 'Before the Storm' are concerned primarily with the RAF during the last decade of peace in Europe, it is important to recall that Britain still had a responsibility to defend its Empire and Dominions. At a time of Nazi ascendency, with all its implications, the British Government also grew increasingly concerned about the growing threat from Fascist Italy as it strived to dominate the central Mediterranean and Horn of Africa region, either of which would later pose a threat to Britain's lines of communication to India and beyond. Mussolini, like Hitler, had also recognized an unwillingness amongst the international community to confront acts of military aggression. Meanwhile, Imperial Japan continued to pursue its belligerent interests far beyond their borders and those areas of mainland China already subjugated in Japan's quest for regional domination and natural resources. Thus, Japan too presented a major concern for Britain, particularly the defence of Australia, New Zealand, Malaya, Singapore, and Hong Kong.

From the Royal Air Force's perspective – having reached its absolute nadir in terms of manpower and equipment in the years immediately following WWI – a 1923 report to the House of Commons on home defence recognised that Britain's aerial defences needed to be expanded in order to offer a credible level of offensive and defensive security. The optimum figure decided upon was for 52 home-based squadrons – 17 fighter and 35 bomber, but *nine* years later the expansion had risen to just 42 squadrons with 490 aircraft, one third of which were allocated to non-regular and cadre units.

By the time the League of Nation's Disarmament Conference convened in 1932, the British Government's despairing policy was that if Britain herself did not re-arm, then the other nations represented at the Conference might follow Britain's example on moral grounds and out of respect for her own self-imposed sacrifice. They didn't.

As for air forces specifically, Britain's ranking in the world frontline air-strength league fell to fifth place behind those of France, the USSR, USA and Italy. Because of the Government's policy, the 52-squadron scheme of 1923 was halted and didn't reach its intended total. The under strength RAF would have to remain so. Adding to the nation's woe was the fact that Britain was in the midst of a deep financial crisis, hence Britain's lack of military expansion was in part explained by economic and not just political or pacifist considerations alone – yet the same financial crisis also gripped Europe and the USA too!

Britain, as with other nations, gained knowledge of Germany's military resurgence from early 1934. Although concerns were expressed internationally as Germany began to expand its armed forces, they were further enhanced once details began to emerge regarding the resurrection of a German air force – the Luftwaffe being *officially* created on 26 February 1935.

In Britain, despite ongoing financial concerns and general pacifistic beliefs, the news caused the government to re-examine its defence policies in general and the parlous state of the RAF in particular. In May 1934, the Cabinet was moved to state - '...the accumulated evidence that Germany has started to rearm in earnest...' required the government to realise '...it would be unsafe to delay the initiation of steps to provide for the safety of the country'. In retrospect it may be said that Britain's initial, sometimes faltering, rearmament programme for all three services dates from this time. More specifically, from the RAF's perspective, the MP, (Prime Minister from 7 June 1935 to 28 May 1937), Stanley Baldwin stated to the Manchester Guardian on 12 June 1934. 'We could simply not avoid increasing our air force'. He specified that the rise of a new Germany had altered for the worse the situation in Europe and that the government could not take risks '...it was the trustee for the people of the country, and it had got to have an

Above:
Fury I K2900 'K' belonging to 1 Squadron as seen during the unit's tour of Canada in 1934. *Carl Vincent*

adequate means of defence, as far as those could be provided' In mid-1934, these comments may be seen to indicate a need for more bombing aircraft.

Accordingly, in July 1934, Scheme 'A' was approved by the Cabinet, it was the first in a series of alphabetically listed aircraft expansion schemes designed firstly to enable Britain to overtake the German lead in military aircraft construction, (already *believed* to be numerically superior to the RAF), and secondly, to dissuade Hitler from any hostile acts or policies towards Britain. By 1935 the stated intention was to demonstrate Britain's ability to out-build Germany 'keel for keel' as it was then phrased, bringing with it a distant echo of the pre-WWI naval arms race when both countries had sought to build dreadnoughts, once the measure of military power prior to the arrival of military aviation.

That the expansion schemes failed in their strictest sense, i.e. they neither overtook the Luftwaffe's lead nor deterred Hitler from his hostile intent is now obvious, but they did allow the RAF to become at least adequately prepared for war in 1939 and certainly to a far greater extent than it had been in September 1938. Churchill summed up the reality even earlier, in 1937, by stating '…the paramount fact remained that the Germans had the lead of us in the air, and also over the whole field of munitions production…' He continued 'It was no longer in our power to forestall Hitler or to regain air parity. Nothing could now prevent the German Army and the German Air Force from becoming the strongest in Europe…we could only improve our position. We could not cure it'.

Churchill's understanding of the extent of Hitler's rearmament was not based solely upon his own knowledge or reports circulated in the press, he had other sources. In early 1936 he had apparently been privy to information from a highly placed Government official (whose identity was not divulged) that

Germany was to spend the equivalent of a 'thousand million pounds sterling' during the year on armaments, a staggering sum of money in 1936, representing approximately half of their combined spend for 1933, 1934 and 1935. That this sum later proved to be exaggerated is irrelevant; what mattered at the time was the perception it was true. These figures caused a stir when Churchill revealed them in the Commons later in the year to the then Chancellor of the Exchequer, Neville Chamberlain. Chamberlain (PM from 28 May 1937) did not dispute the figures but entertained an element of doubt and caution with regard to them. Suffice it to say, Churchill's words, plus those of other like-minded politicians and senior RAF officers, did have an impact in convincing the Treasury to begin loosening its purse strings despite subsequent allegations that they (meaning Churchill mostly) were being overly dramatic and pessimistic with regard to the Luftwaffe's true strength!

Tensions increase – the threat is realised

Space precludes an elaborate explanation of the RAF's expansion program from 1934 to 1939, or the practical and political methods by which it was achieved – all have been addressed by historians and academics far better qualified than the present authors to explain such matters. That said, attention must be drawn to two critical changes in policy made during the RAF's expansion years.

1) Following WWI, Britain and other nations followed an accepted doctrine espousing the dominance in future wars of the bomber and its ability to always defeat the aerial defences of the target country – often summed up by repeating Stanley Baldwin's assertion in his 'A Fear for the Future' speech of 1932 that '…the bomber will always get through'. This led to a larger proportion of financial resources being directed toward the bomber as opposed to defending fighters at a time when technology seemed unable to provide a meaningful performance advantage to the fighter over the night bomber or contemporary light bombers that often outpaced existing interceptors. Yet by 1935 the bombers' seemingly unassailable position looked set to be usurped as a new era of high-performance, low-wing monoplane fighter designs were slowly ushered in.

Lessons were also gleaned during the Spanish Civil War which indicated, Guernica notwithstanding (April 1937), that the effect of bombing cities did not have quite the apocalyptic effect predicted by authors over the previous decade or so. For the cost-conscious British Government this permitted a significant change in policy: instead of fielding an

Below:
As with single-seat fighters, the two-seat Hawker Demon fighter retained many features that hailed from the WWI era, with two open cockpits, fabric covered wings and rear fuselage and a single Lewis gun for the gunner. This anonymous Demon was photographed during the 1938 Munich Crisis period; the recent application of camouflage having erased the fuselage serial number.

armada of expensive, multi-seat, multi-engined bombers with which to deter an enemy, would it not be better to adopt a defensive policy instead? Consequently, in 1937, the Minister for the Co-ordination of Defence – Sir Thomas Inskip – was appointed to examine the situation. In essence, he reoriented British air policy and argued that the RAF's principal role was to defend Great Britain's airspace whilst retaining a viable fleet of bombers should war break out. In Inskip's words the role of the RAF lay not in achieving '... an early knock-out blow, but to prevent the Germans from knocking us out'. In short, financially, Britain was unable to afford a continual aerial arms race with Germany, a race in which Britain already believed itself to be a lot further behind the rest of the field than it actually was. Therefore, an air force comprising more fighters and fewer bombers was a cheaper option.

2) In mid-July 1936, the RAF reorganised itself by eliminating its previous, geographically based, fighting, bombing and coastal areas and instead formed three new commands based on function rather than location. These became respectively: Fighter Command, Bomber Command and Coastal Command and were created under Expansion Scheme 'F' which had been approved five months earlier and allowed for a doubling in size of the RAF by March 1939. (For clarity, the RAF's existing army co-operation units were placed within the purview of Fighter Command for administrative purposes only until, in December 1940, RAF Army Co-Operation Command was created).

Returning to the political and financial questions of the day, 1936 saw the increased promise of modern high-performance monoplane fighters becoming available in the near future with the merest hint that a new radio direction-finding device was being developed. Could the latter, combined with the new fighters, eventually point to an entirely new system of air defence?

Within a fairly short period of time, a progressive chain of strange wooden towers extended along much of the eastern and southern coasts of Britain which would soon become 'force multipliers' in the defence of the nation when its new fighters, and even newer radio direction finding (RDF) techniques were tested to their utmost during the Battle of Britain in 1940. To this day it still stands as one of the few instances in modern military history in which a defensive system was actually used for the purpose it was intended for.

To help appreciate the extent of RAF pre-war expansion it is hoped the aircraft production list will be of benefit, although the figures should be viewed guardedly as they are unlikely to be absolutely precise. They show the quantities of aircraft procured by the Air Ministry (the government department responsible for managing RAF affairs from 1918 to 1964, headed by the Secretary of State for Air) which include training, transport and Fleet Air Arm types as well – the Admiralty didn't regain full control of the FAA until May 1939. It is uncertain if aircraft purchased by Britain from the USA in 1938/39 are included or not, namely the North American Harvard and Lockheed Hudson.

1934: total production		1,110	[549]
1935: total	"	901	[497]
1936: total	"	1,830	[868]
1937: total	"	2,230	[1,301]
1938: total	"	2,831	[1,401]
1939: total	"	7,940	[3,730]

(Presumably the whole of 1939!)
(Figures in brackets show quantity procured for front-line duty)

These figures suggest Britain obtained approximately 16,842 aircraft for military use from 1934 to 1939 of which 8,346 were front-line types. By comparison, the Luftwaffe is believed to have received approximately 29,400 military aircraft in the same period of which perhaps 14,900 were combat aircraft.

By 1930, the House of Commons' 1923 recommendation that the RAF be expanded to include seventeen home-based fighter squadrons had virtually stalled: excluding 54 Squadron then forming (albeit with the Siskin IIIDC), just twelve fighter units existed as yet. Only in 1934 would a further fighter unit, 65 Squadron, be added to Britain's order of battle (OOB), augmented during the year by three Auxiliary Air Force squadrons following receipt of an instruction to switch them from their existing bombing role to that of fighter, despite which, each would have to retain their biplane bombers until Hawker Demon two-seat fighters were made available to them in 1936 and 1937.

(**See Appendix 1:** *RAF Fighter Squadrons and their aircraft 1930 to December 1939*).

Above:
Gloster Gladiator I, K6132 from 72 Squadron seen landing in June 1937. Still of biplane configuration with a fixed undercarriage, the Gladiator introduced an enclosed cockpit, flaps, internally sprung mainwheels, and a doubling of the heretofore twin fixed Vickers gun armament to four Browning machine guns. 72 Squadron operated the Gladiator from February 1937 to May 1939, and then again in March 1940 for two weeks when their airfield at Acklington became so waterlogged their Spitfires were unable to operate. *Tony O'Toole*

Another unit, 74 Squadron, re-formed in late 1935 while en route to Malta in response to increasing political tensions in the Mediterranean created by Mussolini, his ongoing war against Ethiopia (Abyssinia as it was then generally referred to by Europeans), and the total impotence of the League of Nations.

During the course of 1936, as the political climate in Western Europe also became increasingly tense, four further RAF fighter squadrons re-formed – it was also the year in which the complete reorganisation of the RAF's operational structure commenced when the previous geographically-based operating structure was replaced by the Command system i.e., Fighter, Bomber and Coastal Commands.

By September 1938, RAF Fighter Command had begun to receive monoplane fighters and was gaining operational efficiency. Four squadrons were by this time equipped with Hawker Hurricanes with one more (85 Squadron) currently receiving them. (Two more were scheduled to receive Hurricanes in October.) Meanwhile, 19 Squadron had become the RAF's first Supermarine Spitfire unit one month earlier, although it retained Gloster Gauntlets until March 1939.

Thus, of the six units referred to, only Hurricane-equipped 56, 73, 87 and 111 Squadrons were operational. Otherwise, Britain's fighter defences remained an all-biplane force comprising nine squadrons of Gauntlets, six with Gloster Gladiators (excluding two others in the Middle East), eight with Hawker Demons and three with Hawker Furies – all of which had been decidedly outflown by Bristol Blenheim bombers during a series of air exercises held a year earlier in 1937.

There is no doubt that the eleven months following Munich proved as valuable to Fighter Command as it did to the rest of the RAF and Britain's armed forces as a whole. However, a lot more was required beyond simply creating further frontline squadrons: existing units had to be sustained and replenished; increasing numbers of pilots and groundcrew had to be trained, and substantial material reserves established. Even though much was accomplished, it would be wrong to assume that by 3 September 1939 all

home-based front line biplane fighter units had been swept away given that four Gladiator squadrons remained; so too, nominally at least, did two Gauntlet squadrons. As Hurricane and Spitfire numbers continued to grow through the late autumn as the expansion process continued, an additional three home-based fighter squadrons were formed each equipped with Gladiators. By October or November 1939, it is estimated that the RAF fielded 115 operational Gladiators with perhaps thirty-five more in reserve, although these quantities probably included Gladiators based in the Middle East as well as at home.

At the end of December, the RAF's (fighter) order of battle comprised eighteen Hurricane, fourteen Spitfire, eighteen Blenheim If, one Blenheim IVf and four Gladiator squadrons, plus 264 Squadron then receiving the Boulton Paul Defiant turret fighter, although in no sense was the latter operational. While the numbers initially appear quite respectable, the twin-engined Blenheims inclusion in the OOB should cast a note of caution inasmuch that as a fighter its value was restricted primarily to patrolling over coastal and North Sea convoy traffic to deter Luftwaffe anti-shipping patrols. History would soon reveal the Blenheims vulnerability to modern fighters.

At this point it might be worth explaining that the term Fighter Command referred to the RAF's Regular fighter units which, by summer 1939, consisted of twenty-five squadrons, a number that obviously fluctuated in the following weeks as further squadrons formed or re-formed. Additionally, fourteen Auxiliary Air Force fighter squadrons also existed at this time albeit several were awaiting delivery of modern equipment. *

To clarify, commencing with 502 Squadron on 15 May 1925, five Special Reserve units were formed numbered 500 to 504 Squadrons inclusive. These were bomber units and they remained so until all five were transferred to the Auxiliary Air Force (AAF) in 1936 (1937 in 502's case).

Almost simultaneously, starting with 602 Squadron in September 1925, the RAF was further augmented by the formation of regionally based AAF Squadrons. These units were numbered 600 to 605 and 607 to 616 Squadrons. 616 Squadron was initiated on 1 November 1938 following the renumbering of 503 Squadron, while 613 became the last AAF unit to form in March 1939. The number 606 was not taken up. Not all AAF units transitioned to the fighter role. (See Appendix 1).

The Auxiliary Air Force would receive the prefix 'Royal' from King George VI in 1947 to honour its achievements in WWII.

Below:
Excluding the Bristol M.IC monoplane fighter which served the RAF until the last of its type was withdrawn by 63 Squadron in December 1919, the Hawker Hurricane became the first monoplane fighter to enter operational service with the RAF. This photo shows prototype K5083 complete with enclosed cockpit, fabric covered wings and rear fuselage, eight Browning machine guns (ultimately), plus its short-lived D-shaped inner wheel covers.

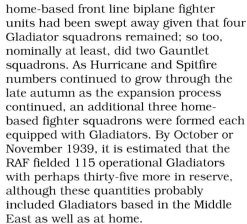

RAF biplane fighters: 1930-1939

Armstrong Whitworth Siskin IIIA

An improved Siskin III, the IIIA's most obvious external differences when compared to its predecessor was a revised fin and rudder that did away with the ventral tailfin, and the Jaguar III engine, the latter being replaced by the more powerful Jaguar IV and, later, the supercharged IVA to improve overall performance above 10,000ft.

It is thought the first Jaguar IV-powered Siskin IIIA to fly was J8428 which made its first flight on 21 October 1925 but there's a possibility it was 'pipped' by J8048 which might have made its maiden flight a day earlier! J8048 was the first production airframe from the first production batch (J8048 to J8060) – all thirteen being issued to 111 Squadron commencing in September 1926 to replace their existing Siskin IIIs while simultaneously becoming the first Siskin IIIA squadron. Thereafter the IIIA continued to enter squadron service in the following sequence: 1, 41 and 56 Squadrons in 1927; 17, 19, 29, 32 and 43

Below:
Taken in 1928 or 1929, these Siskin IIIAs belonged to Northolt-based 41 Squadron. The unit's colours, consisting of a solid red bar along the full length of the fuselage and spanwise across the upper mainplane, are readily visible in this image although their fuselage serial numbers are anything but, due no doubt because they were applied to the red bar using Aluminium paint. Whilst the two machines furthest from the camera remain unidentified, the leader is J8830 with J8948 positioned aft on the leader's port wing, while J8657 flies at the rear (nearest the camera). Of the trio it would appear that J8948 might have survived the longest as it was apparently allocated to the Andover Communication Flight in February 1932, following which there is no further record of either the Flight itself or J8948.

Above:
Seen in late 1926, Siskin IIIA, J8057, was one of the initial batch of thirteen production airframes all of which went to 111 Squadron in September 1926, making this one of the earliest images to show a IIIA in RAF service – unfortunate pose notwithstanding. Whereas J8057 survived this incident, its luck ran out in September 1927 when it suffered a mid-air collision and was written off. Finished in overall Aluminium with a dark grey panel behind the cockpit, 111 Squadron colours consisted of a single black bar along each side of the fuselage with another between the roundels on the upper wing.

Top right:
Siskin IIIA J8964 was a 32 Squadron machine as indicated by the interrupted blue bar along its fuselage (repeated on the upper mainplane) forward of the roundel and continuing as a solid blue bar aft of the roundel to the tailplane. Photographed in 1928 or 1929, IIIA J8850 from the same unit sits in the background. J8964 went to 29 Squadron in June 1929 before being allocated to 3 FTS where it served until 24 June 1931, the day it crashed near Ketton, Rutland. J8850 left 32 Squadron in April 1929 and was written off following a crash two months later.

Centre:
Siskin IIIA J8933, belonging to 29 Squadron, was a Gloster-built machine as characterised by the curving font of the serial number. J8933 served with 29 Squadron from March 1928 to October 1929 and displays the unit's two parallel red bars separated by three red 'X-type' characters positioned forward of the fuselage roundel; similarly six 'X's were applied to the upper mainplane. As can be seen the underwing roundel overlaps the aileron while in the background, third from the camera, the forward fuselage of a Bristol F.2B is evident.

Bottom right:
Photographed in 1929, Siskin IIIA J9355 joined 17 Squadron in September 1928 and remained until October 1929 when Bulldog IIs replaced the Siskins. Here, J9355's fuselage zigzags extend only as far as the roundel, but whether this applied to all their Siskins isn't clear. (See Woodcock J7960 for description of the unit's markings.)

Squadrons in 1928; followed by 25 Squadron in March 1929 *(for dates and length of squadron service see Appendix 1)*. The only apparent anomaly concerns 54 Squadron. This unit did indeed receive Siskins in January 1930, but, as the reader will recall, they received the Siskin III(DC) pending arrival of Bulldogs later that year.

How many Siskin IIIAs were manufactured? The answer is unclear, not least because some sources include new-build III(DC)s and the thirty-plus converted III(DC)s in with the IIIA total.

Seemingly, the number of single-seat IIIAs actually ordered by the Air Ministry from June 1926 onwards amounts to an impressive 340 airframes (including J8428), the majority of which entered RAF service over the next few years. However, this figure does not include two that were converted from a III to IIIA (there were probably more), nor does it include eight IIIAs and two III(DC)s supplied to the RCAF of which two, J8632 and J8633, were supplied from RAF stock and replaced by new-build airframes utilizing the same serials.†

Right:
Built by Vickers, Siskin IIIA J9876 belonged to 1 Squadron which re-formed in February 1927 and operated the type until February 1932, with J9876 being delivered new to the unit in February 1930. Presumably this photo was taken after August 1930 when implementation of the new rudder stripe sequence, with red leading, was introduced. Points of interest are the replacement rudder, taken from J8947, and what appears to be a yellow fin (possibly denoting B Flight), which looks dark when orthochromatic film is used. Being blue sensitive, the film was easily overexposed making anything blue look pale and turning anything yellow or red much darker, causing the red in the roundel and the squadron's two red bars look significantly darker than the blue.

The candidate for the RAF's last flying Siskin was probably IIIA J8942 which was on charge with the Aircraft Training Station at Digby in 1938, its ultimate fate is apparently unknown. Otherwise, a couple of late-surviving airworthy RAF Siskins are known to have existed into 1936. Occasional reference is made to the Siskin IIIB, of which one certainly existed; IIIA, J8627, was experimentally fitted with a Jaguar VIII radial engine in October 1928 before trialling and testing other engines until July 1931 when it disappears from the record. One source, however, considers that a late batch of IIIAs (J9897 to J9911) were actually IIIBs, possibly because they were fitted with a Jaguar IVA from the outset. Just to stir muddied waters further, we might ponder the designation given to at least two IIIAs

that were converted to dual-control trainers. Did they become the Mk.IIIA(DC)? One wonders.

† *Surviving RCAF Siskins represented the country's entire fighter force until Hurricanes were received in early 1939, at which point the Siskins were placed in store. At the start of the war five IIIA's were taken out of storage for use as instructional airframes A26 to A30. Two were written off after a couple of years while the other three appear to have been issued to other organizations, but all had gone for scrap before the end of WWII. The long-held belief that three Siskins remained in service at war's end can be attributed to bureaucracy which demanded they would remain on RCAF strength until someone got around to formally striking them off charge at a later date.*

Top left:
Armstrong Whitworth Siskin IIIA, J9901 of 19 Squadron, based at RAF Duxford, c.1930. The aircraft carries 19 Squadron's blue and white checks on the fuselage forward of the roundel, as well as between the roundels on the upper wing. It appears too that the rudder striping has been amended with red leading. Note that Siskins carried roundels in the 1-2-3 ratio in all positions, albeit that, being a sesquiplane, they were positioned under the top wing rather than under the lower one which simply featured the serial number. The hyphen between the letter and the first numeral of the serial was common to all Siskins whether Armstrong Whitworth, Blackburn, Bristol, Gloster or Vickers built. The lettering on the tyre reads 'PALMER CORD AERO TYRE'. Other than joining 19 Squadron on 14 March 1930, little more is known about J9901.

Bottom left:
Operated by 32 Squadron from April 1928, followed by 29 and 1 Squadrons, Siskin IIIA, J8959 was reconditioned and modified by Vickers in late 1929 prior to being allocated to 43 Squadron at Tangmere in June 1930 and in whose markings it is seen here while being flown by S/Ldr C N Lowe. The unit's black and white checks were carried on the fuselage forward of the roundel, on the fin and, though difficult to see here, on both surfaces of the elevator as well as across the span of the upper mainplane between the roundels. The rudder striping has been updated with red leading. From 1927 to 1931, Lowe led the squadron's aerobatic team which thrilled the crowds attending the Hendon pageants with their low-flying formations – while literally tied together with bunting at the 1930 event. However, in May 1931, the squadron became the first to receive the Hawker Fury I and the Siskin's days became numbered. Shortly afterwards J8959 was transferred to 5 FTS with which it remained until at least the following November.

Above:
As many readers will know, operational aircraft types were and still are allocated to specific training units in order to bring aircrew up to the level of skill required to operate contemporary aircraft effectively. Here a trio of Siskin IIIAs from 3 FTS are seen in the early nineteen thirties led by Gloster-built J9335 with J9336 '2' to starboard and Bristol-built J9329 to port (nearest the camera). While J9335 and J9336 both served with 3 FTS from September 1929 to March 1932, J9329 only served with the unit from the second half of 1930 until March 1932. Re-formed at Spittlegate, Lincolnshire, on 1 April 1928, 3 FTS was initially equipped with the Avro 504N, Siskin III and IIIA plus supporting aircraft including one or two Grebes (J7383 was one) and Gamecocks (possibly J8089). These were subsequently replaced by Avro Tutors, Armstrong Whitworth Atlases and Hawker Hart variants supplemented by Bulldog IIAs and Furies.

Below:
Built by Blackburn, J8869 is seen while serving with 24 Squadron (a government transport, communications and training unit) which re-formed at Kenley in February 1920; the training element being provided to enable Air Ministry pilots to remain current on their respective types. J8869 remained with 24 Squadron from December 1930 until the following July when it was transferred to the CFS at RAF Upavon, Wiltshire. Other than a black '24' denoting the squadron, the only other marking is a broad chevron on the fin comprising of two red horizontal chevrons separated by a single blue one, a motif that was retained by the unit until the mid-to-late 1930s.

Bristol Bulldog II/IIA/TM

Lulled into a false sense of security by French bombers such as the Farman Goliath and others, few of which could exceed 110 mph at any altitude, Britain's cash-strapped government of the mid-1920s was happy (as indeed it is today) to entertain significant complacency when pondering the nation's fighter defences at a time when France was the only potential enemy. Air Ministry policy appeared to confirm that all was well and that the existing Grebes and shortly to arrive Gamecocks and Siskin IIIAs would remain viable given their performance advantage over French bombers.

All seemed well until, in 1925, a new two-seat light bomber, the Fairey Fox, flew for the first time and existing attitudes in respect of Britain's fighter defences were rudely shattered. Powered by a streamlined 480hp inline Curtiss D.12

engine, the Fox transformed British thinking given that it was quite capable of outpacing contemporary fighters. The latter point was brusquely emphasised when 12 Squadron, having re-equipped with the type in June 1926, made full use of their 156 mph bomber to evade all fighter defences in the 1928 air exercises. (A lesson that would be repeated again when Harts and Blenheim bombers entered service.)

The implication was obvious, the advanced Fox meant that both the Siskin IIIA and Gamecock were already on the brink of obsolescence, thus a replacement was required to replace both as soon as possible. Consequently, in 1928, the Air Ministry selected the Bristol Aeroplane Company's private venture Type 105 Bulldog as a counter to the fast light bomber.

Ignoring its fairly tortuous development

Above:
One of the first batch of twenty-five Bulldog IIs, J9574 served with 3 Squadron from June 1929 until 12 June 1930 when it collided with a 100 Squadron Hawker Horsley over Upavon while practising for an RAF display and was written off. Carrying the squadron's emerald green bar along the fuselage side, from engine to rudder post and between the roundels on the upper wing, J9574 is seen in 1929 with ground crew helping the aircraft to taxi prior to departing for a summer exercise.

Left:
Another 3 Squadron Bulldog II from the first production batch, one which better illustrates their emerald green bar along the length of the fuselage. The fuselage spine was dark green while the mainwheel hubs are thought to have been red, possibly denoting A Flight. J9576 joined the unit on 4 July 1929 and remained until November 1930 when it crashed requiring a return to the makers for repairs. Photographed before the rudder stripe sequence was reversed, this image clearly shows the engine's valve gear covers which were not fitted to the Mk.IIA.

Top right:
Bulldog IIA, K1676, is seen while serving with 23 Squadron just prior to taking part in an air exercise at RAF Kenley on 21 July 1931. Interestingly, the fuselage serial number is displayed on an Aluminium rectangle within the unit's alternating red and blue fuselage band, colours that were repeated on the upper mainplane. The elevators and mainwheel hub covers appear to be red – possibly denoting the A Flight leader and, as with the unit's earlier Gamecocks, the squadron badge, an eagle preying on a falcon with the Latin motto Semper Aggressus on a yellow scroll appears on the fin.

Bottom right:
A formation of 17 Squadron's Bulldog II/IIAs in June 1930. When 17 Squadron exchanged its Siskins for Bulldogs in October 1929, it inherited aircraft from co-located 3 Squadron resulting for a time in a varied mix of unit colours as this photo amply demonstrates. On the far side Bulldog II, J9587, wears a full set of 17 Squadron black zig-zag markings on both the fuselage as well as the upper wing, in contrast the lead aircraft Mk.IIA K1081 carries 3 Squadron's emerald green bars on its upper wing with 17 Squadron markings along its fuselage, while nearest the camera Bulldog IIA K1085 simply carries 3 Squadron bars on its upper wing. Of the three, J9587 was reconditioned in September 1930 and joined 29 Squadron in 1932; K1081 collided with a Bulldog II on 6 May 1931 during an attack on a bomber formation and crashed, while K1085 flew into the ground in fog in September 1930 and was SOC.

path which need not be recited here, the prototype Bulldog II (Type 105A) was allocated the serial J9480 and made its first flight on 21 January 1928. The first unit to receive the type was 3 Squadron whose first examples arrived in May 1929, the transition from Gamecock to Bulldog II being completed in July. Thereafter Bulldogs continued to enter squadron service in the following sequence: 17 Squadron in 1929; 54 and 32 in 1930; 111, 23, 19 and 41 in 1931; 29 and 56 Squadrons in 1932. *(See Appendix 1)*.

Powered by a Jupiter VII radial engine, forty-eight Bulldog IIs were supplied to the RAF before production switched to the more numerous IIA. The latter featured a Jupiter VIIF radial as well as revisions to the airframe itself and a strengthened wider undercarriage to cope with the resultant increase in all-up weight. In 1933, most surviving Bulldog IIAs received a modified fin, Dunlop disc wheels and a castoring tailwheel in lieu of a tail skid.

Air Ministry orders for single-seat Bulldogs:
25 x Mk.II del from 4.29
(J9567 - J9591)
23 x Mk.II del 1.30 to 5.30
(K1079 - K1101)

Mk.IIA production:
92 x Mk.IIA del 10.30 to 5.31
(K1603 - K1694)
100 x Mk.IIA del 7.31 to 4.32
(K2135 - K2234) K2188 was completed as prototype two-seat TM
20 x Mk.IIA del 4.32 to 7.32
(K2476 - K2495)
14 x Mk.IIA del 7.32 to 12.32
(K2859 - K2872)
18 x Mk.IIA del 4.33 to 6.33
(K2946 - K2963)
10 x Mk.IIA del 6.33 to 11.33
(K3504 - K3513)

Left:
Bulldog IIAs from 111 Squadron on a misty day in late 1932. All the aircraft carry the unit's single black tapering bar on the fuselage which extended aft from the cockpit and terminated at the rudder hinge obscuring their serials which otherwise only appeared on the rudder and lower mainplane. A parallel black bar was also applied to the upper wing between the roundels forward of which, in this instance at least, each fighter has a camera gun fitted attached to brackets located to the left of the pilot's forward line of vision. Of the four Bulldogs seen here three can be identified. The nearest, K1625, was delivered to 111 Squadron on 2 February 1931 and remained with them until joining 2 ASU in January 1935. It was SOC six months later. The second airframe, K1683, joined 111 Squadron in April 1931 and survived until 5 May 1936 when it stalled and crashed into the river Nene killing the pilot. Third from the camera is K2208 which force landed, overturned and was damaged beyond repair at Northolt on 6 May 1936.

Bulldog TM:
The Air Ministry also ordered two-seat Bulldog TMs to replace the Siskin III(DC).
17 x TM del 12.32 to 3.33
(K3170 - K3186)
31 x TM del 10.33 to 5.34
(K3923 - K3953)
Eleven further TMs (**K4566 - K4576**) were also procured. All were delivered to 1 Aircraft Storage Unit (ASU) in March 1935 where they remained until disposed of en masse on 25 November 1937.

Excluding prototype J9480, the figures indicate that the number of military Bulldogs acquired by the Air Ministry for all purposes amounts to 302 single seat Bulldog II/IIAs (K2188 included for clarity) plus 59 production Bulldog TM airframes. *
* *Additionally, Mk.IIA, K4189 was ordered as a static airframe to test stainless steel construction. The Air Ministry also accepted Bulldog IV, G-ABZW, which became K4292 for use by the A&AEE in 1933, becoming 1180M in November 1938.*

Seemingly remembered with more affection and nostalgia than any other British interwar biplane fighter (probably more than it actually deserves despite its undoubted agility and reliability), such affection should not be allowed to mask the fact that the Bulldog was outclassed by 1933. While the era of the two-gun, radial engined, single-seat open-cockpit fighter was not quite over, technology – exemplified by the Rolls-Royce Kestrel engine for example – was moving on apace.

For a few years Bulldogs formed the backbone of Britain's fighter defences. Ten RAF squadrons ultimately operated the type, although this total was only briefly achieved between October 1932 and April 1933 when 23 Squadron's remaining Bulldogs gave way to the Hawker Demon. In 1936, six squadrons were still equipped with the now obsolete Bulldog, although it was 1937 before 3 Squadron, the first to operate the type, also became the last when, commencing in March 1937, their now thoroughly obsolete mounts were replaced by the Gloster Gladiator I.

While several Bulldogs continued to serve for a time with training units or meteorological flights, most of the remaining airframes appear to have been sent to 2 or 4 Aircraft Storage Unit to await final disposal which seems to have occurred in July and August 1938. Even then a few lingered on as instructional airframes, the longest lived probably being Mk.IIA K2957 which became 1149M in October 1938, then 2184M in August 1940.

Above:
Seen in 1931, this formation of 19 Squadron Bulldog IIAs display their prominent 72 inch diameter wing roundels to advantage. The aircraft leading the 'vic' on the right of the photo is thought to have been S/Ldr A G Sanderson's machine, K2159, which featured blue and white checks on the fin and both surfaces of the elevator as well as the fuselage sides and upper mainplanes. K2159 also carried a squadron leader's pennant on both sides of the rudder just above the serial number. At least two of the other Bulldogs appear to have darker fins, which may have been red (A Flight) and yellow (B Flight) indicating Flight Leaders' machines.

Top right:
Devoid of rudder markings, Bulldog IIA K1606 was amongst the first of its Mark to enter service, which makes this image interesting in that it displays some of the external modifications applied to surviving Mk.IIAs in 1933. These included: a castoring tailwheel in lieu of a tailskid, Dunlop disc wheels and an enlarged fin. Further alterations included the replacement of the type's original 'narrow' track undercarriage with a wider one, plus in some instances, the fitting of external cartridge collection boxes – a detail not applicable to K1606 as they seem only to have been fitted to 17 and 56 Squadron machines, although, as ever, exceptions would have existed. By the time this photo was taken, K1606 had been with 32 Squadron since March 1932 and probably remained with the unit until July 1936 when their ageing Bulldogs were replaced by Gloster Gauntlet IIs. On 23 November 1936, K1606 became instructional airframe 905M. The unit's colours consisted of a blue fuselage band interrupted by two diagonal breaks, while the band on the upper wing was interrupted with three diagonal breaks. The black fuselage serial was outlined in Aluminium and the motif on the fin is that of Bristol's own bulldog logo.

Bulldogs were fitted with two heated Vickers .303 Mk.II* (* = 'star') machine guns with 600 rounds per gun (rpg), an Aldis gun sight and a 4½ diameter ring- and-bead sight, the latter located to the left of the fuselage centre line and the Aldis to the right. Four 20lb HE bombs could be carried under the lower left wing.

Above:
As related, a two-seat training variant of the Bulldog fighter was developed and called the Bulldog TM; K3172 was from the first batch of TMs to be delivered between December 1932 and March 1933. Having served with the RAF College (RAFC) Cranwell for two years, K3172's last posting was to Demon-equipped 41 Squadron in March 1936 coded 'A'. Eight months later K3172 was serving with 1 SoTT as instructional airframe 910M. Other than the seating arrangement the main differences between the Bulldog IIA and TM was the latter's wider undercarriage, larger fin and rudder, and a 3½ degree sweepback on both the upper and lower wings.

Below:
This interesting photo was taken at one of the many suburban airfields that once formed a ring around London and so it is assumed these Mk.IIAs, with K21xx closest to the camera, were participating in one of the many air exercises conducted in the mid-1930s. These are RAF machines all of which display the extended fin, Dunlop main wheels and new tailwheel associated with the modifications introduced from 1933. As can be seen, all national and unit markings have been temporarily obscured, although the first and third examples retain evidence of a solid broad band along their upper wings. Close inspection shows that these Bulldogs have been fitted with external cartridge collection boxes – seen as a slight bulge behind and below the gun trough and below the cockpit – a detail applied primarily to 17 and 56 Squadron examples – but not necessarily exclusively as neither unit employed a single-colour solid band on the upper wing by this time.

Hawker Fury I/II

Developed by Hawker, the Fury was chosen as a specialised interceptor to meet the twin requirements of speed and the ability to climb quickly to altitude. The first production Fury I, K1926, made its maiden flight on 25 March 1931 and was followed by 117 further examples for the RAF.

The type entered operational service in May 1931 when it replaced 43 Squadron's Siskin IIIAs at Tangmere, West Sussex, an airfield located close to the south coast and thus well placed to take advantage of the new fighter's performance. Due, presumably, to tight budgetary constraints at the time only two other RAF squadrons would receive the Fury I which replaced Siskins with 1 Squadron at

Tangmere and 25 Squadron at Hawkinge in February 1932.

Given there was not as yet a system in place that could reliably detect the early approach of hostile aircraft as they departed the European mainland, the only warning would be the increasing tempo of aircraft engines as they neared the English coastline to the south or south-east of London. The Fury's role, therefore, as a fast-climbing interceptor, was to engage the enemy as they crossed the southern coast, the hope being that the more numerous but slower Bulldogs based further inland towards London would have time to gain sufficient altitude to attack the enemy before they reached the capital.

Right:
A line up of 43 Squadron Fury Is seen at the 1935 Hendon Display with K1942 displaying the unit's black and Aluminium chequered markings forward of the fuselage roundel (and repeated on the upper mainplane). Originally K1942 would have been delivered with rudder stripes applied, but by 1935 they had been removed and replaced with plain Aluminium-doped rudder fabric. K1942's mainwheel hubs were probably yellow, denoting a B Flight machine. Having become the first to equip with the Fury I, 43 Squadron also became the last to use them operationally, their last examples being surrendered in late January 1939. K1942 became instructional airframe 749M in January 1936.

Bottom right:
Fury I, K2078, served with 25 Squadron throughout its active life until relegated to instructional airframe status in February 1937 as 948M. This photo was probably taken in 1934/1935 as all the aircraft seen here appear to have replacement rudders (in a slightly darker/fresher V84 Aluminium finish) devoid of rudder stripes. Each aircraft carries the squadron motif consisting of a hawk on a gauntlet with the unit's motto Feriens Tego (Striking I Defend) on a yellow scroll. The unit's colours consisted of two black parallel bars forward of the fuselage roundel which tapered to meet aft of the serial number; two parallel black bars were applied to the upper wing from roundel to roundel.

Above:
Belonging to 1 Squadron RAF, Fury I K2878 'L' was photographed during the Squadron's tour of Canada in 1934. By March 1937 K2878 was in use with 87 Squadron (a Fury II unit) before being passed to 11 FTS who operated it until 1 March 1938 when it crash-landed and was SOC. The bowser carries the words 'AEROPLANE SPIRIT' and 'AIRPORT SERVICE ST-HUBERT'. *Carl Vincent*

Right:
Photographed during 1 Squadron's tour of Canada in 1934, K2900 was one of six Fury Is delivered at a time when rudder stripes were still being applied. Allocated to 1 Squadron on 28 May 1934 and coded 'K', this aircraft served with the unit throughout its life which ended in November 1937 when its undercarriage collapsed while landing at Tangmere. The aircraft's individual aircraft letter 'K' can be seen on the brightly polished natural metal cowling panels that contrast with the V84 Aluminium finish on the fabric areas. K2900's rudder stripes and roundels are in the Bright Red VR3 and Bright Blue VB2 shades which, due to the use of orthochromatic film, makes the red look darker than the blue. The squadron bars are also Bright Red VR3. K2900's fin stripes were probably removed in October 1935 when it made a temporary visit to the Henlow HAD. *Carl Vincent*

Right:
Another view of 1 Squadron's Furies during their visit to Canada in June and July 1934. K2901 joined 1 Squadron in May 1934 and remained with the unit until it collided with K2902 on 17 December 1937 killing both pilots. The second Fury in line is K2074 'J' which was destroyed when it broke up performing aerobatics in October 1937 when serving with 43 Squadron. The aircraft at the end of the line is a Ford Trimotor. *Carl Vincent*

Powered by a 525hp Kestrel IIS, the Fury was the first RAF fighter in squadron service to exceed 200 mph in level flight (207 mph at 14,000ft), giving it a comfortable edge over contemporary heavy bomber designs, but less so over the modern Hawker Hart two-seat light bomber's maximum speed of 184 mph. In order to successfully intercept them the Furies would need to be precisely positioned to achieve this, a factor that would ultimately lead to the development of an efficient ground controlled interception system.

Fury I squadrons were intended to blunt the impact of bombers sent from France to bomb London. In 1932, France still remained Britain's only potential enemy as it alone, among other European states, possessed a bomber force that might conceivably be capable of mounting a serious attack on the capital. Hence, for the purposes of operational defence planning, France remained the 'enemy' for the time being! Unfortunately, the Fury, for all its elegance and speed, hid a flaw not of its making – unreliable guns. They were a constant source of frustration for pilots who consistently filed reports about gun stoppages and other faults relating to the Vickers machine gun, especially at higher

altitudes. Given the miniscule number of Fury squadrons available, and the significance of their task, repeated stoppages proved to be a considerable irritation for all concerned. The faults were not confined to the Fury alone it must be said as most other user types suffered similarly. While the Vickers gun would remain an excellent infantry weapon for another three decades and had proved to be generally reliable in the air during WWI, it was the post-war attempts to improve the rate of fire for airborne use that caused the stoppages. (See 'Gladiator gun progression – From Vickers to Browning' below).

Luckily, in the event, RAF Furies were never called upon to fire their guns in anger, although some ex-RAF machines that were transferred to the South African Air Force (SAAF) did go into action against the Italian air force over East Africa in 1940 and did succeed in shooting down

two, perhaps three, Caproni Ca.133 bomber/transports.

Ongoing development of the Fury I led to the Fury II which employed the 640hp Kestrel VI engine to bestow a 16 mph speed advantage over the Mk.I and, more importantly, reduced the time taken to reach 10,000ft from 4.5 to 3.8 minutes. Armament remained virtually the same albeit the Fury II was fitted with a pair of Vickers Mk.V .303in machine guns. One hundred and twelve Fury IIs were ordered for the RAF, the first being delivered to 9 FTS on 24 July 1936.

Of the three existing Fury I units only 25 Squadron was destined to operate the Mk.II; delivered in October and November 1936 they were used until October 1937, by which time the much faster Blenheim bomber was already in squadron service. Thereafter, 73 Squadron at Mildenhall and

Continued on page 40

Top left:
Remaining in Canada where 1 Squadron's Furies were photographed from above to reveal, from left to right, the upper wing surfaces of K2074, K2900, K2878, K2899 and K2901. *Carl Vincent*

Bottom left:
Seen prior to 28 August 1936, the day K2040 (nearest) hit the ground and was written off, 1 Squadron Fury Is K2040, K2043, K5673 and K2881 formate as part of the unit's 1936 aerobatic team. This photo shows the positioning of the squadron's red bars on the upper mainplane which lined up with the rear of the roundels that had been reduced in size to avoid overlapping the ailerons. Other points of interest include the incomplete serial number on K2040's rudder; the unit motif (a winged numeral '1' on a white background) on K2040 and K2043; while late-production Fury K5673 displays its winged numeral within a white fighter spearhead on the fin, a feature that was becoming a standard marking in 1936. K2043 became 1019M in December 1937; K5673 joined 1 Squadron on 2 June 1936 but was serving with 3 FTS in December 1938 when it stalled on landing, tipped up and was written off; K2881 remained with 1 Squadron until struck by a Fury II at Tangmere on 23 February 1938 becoming 1049M by April.

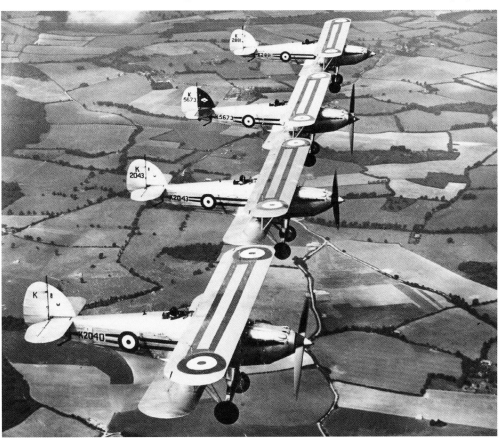

Sopwith 7F1 Snipe E6965, 1 Sqn, RAF Hinaidi, Iraq, spring/summer 1922
No.1 Squadron moved to Hinaidi, Iraq, from Bangalore, India in April 1922. As the post-war need to camouflage aircraft diminished a cellulose-based dope, V84 'Aluminium', was gradually introduced on new airframes or when older aircraft, such as E6965, were re-doped. The forward fuselage metal panels and the cowling remained in either natural polished metal, as illustrated by E6965, or painted a dark grey (Battleship Grey – see profile below). Red/White/Blue roundels were applied in all six positions with rudder striping with Blue nearest the rudder post. By April 1924, E6965 was back in the UK where it served briefly with 41 Squadron prior to joining 19 Squadron. Thereafter E6965 was allocated to a Meteorological Flight in mid-1925 although its ultimate fate is uncertain.

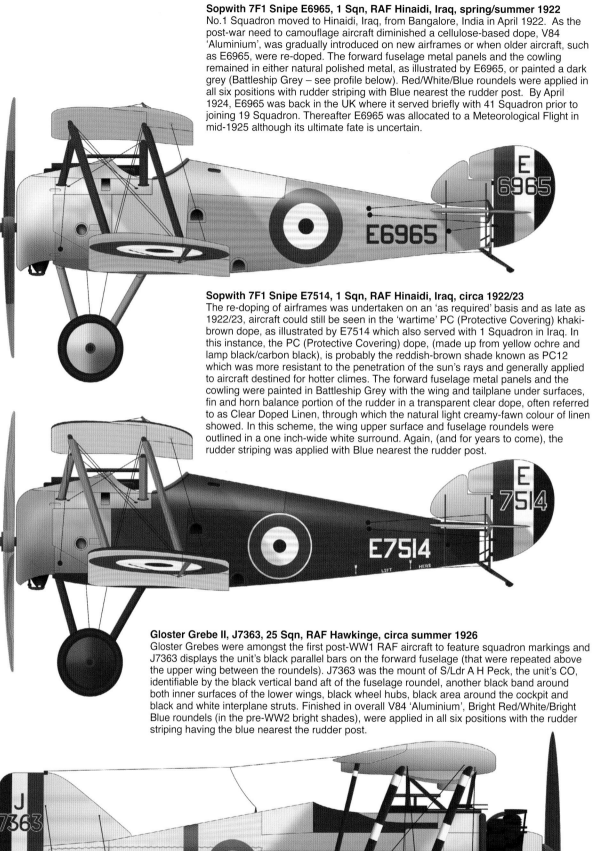

Sopwith 7F1 Snipe E7514, 1 Sqn, RAF Hinaidi, Iraq, circa 1922/23
The re-doping of airframes was undertaken on an 'as required' basis and as late as 1922/23, aircraft could still be seen in the 'wartime' PC (Protective Covering) khaki-brown dope, as illustrated by E7514 which also served with 1 Squadron in Iraq. In this instance, the PC (Protective Covering) dope, (made up from yellow ochre and lamp black/carbon black), is probably the reddish-brown shade known as PC12 which was more resistant to the penetration of the sun's rays and generally applied to aircraft destined for hotter climes. The forward fuselage metal panels and the cowling were painted in Battleship Grey with the wing and tailplane under surfaces, fin and horn balance portion of the rudder in a transparent clear dope, often referred to as Clear Doped Linen, through which the natural light creamy-fawn colour of linen showed. In this scheme, the wing upper surface and fuselage roundels were outlined in a one inch-wide white surround. Again, (and for years to come), the rudder striping was applied with Blue nearest the rudder post.

Gloster Grebe II, J7363, 25 Sqn, RAF Hawkinge, circa summer 1926
Gloster Grebes were amongst the first post-WW1 RAF aircraft to feature squadron markings and J7363 displays the unit's black parallel bars on the forward fuselage (that were repeated above the upper wing between the roundels). J7363 was the mount of S/Ldr A H Peck, the unit's CO, identifiable by the black vertical band aft of the fuselage roundel, another black band around both inner surfaces of the lower wings, black wheel hubs, black area around the cockpit and black and white interplane struts. Finished in overall V84 'Aluminium', Bright Red/White/Bright Blue roundels (in the pre-WW2 bright shades), were applied in all six positions with the rudder striping having the blue nearest the rudder post.

Gloster Grebe II, J7381, 29 Sqn, RAF Duxford, circa 1925/26
When 29 Squadron re-equipped with Gloster Grebes (from Sopwith Snipes) in
September 1925, the overall 'Aluminium' finish had become standard on RAF
Fighters, with Bright Red/White/Bright Blue roundels (in the pre-WW2 bright shades),
in all six positions and rudder striping with the Blue nearest the rudder post. At this
time, the squadron introduced the red 'X's flanked by red bars 'squadron markings'
along the forward fuselage in front of the roundel and spanwise along the upper
mainplanes in between the roundels. The number of red 'X's varied, with four
along the fuselage and five between the upper wing roundels.

Gloster Gamecock I, J8084, 23 Sqn, RAF Henlow, circa 1930
Finished in the now standard overall 'Aluminium' scheme with Bright Red/White/Bright
Blue roundels in all six positions, it will be noticed that the rudder striping now has the
Red nearest the rudder post, a change introduced by the Air Ministry in 1930. 23
Squadron's red and blue bars were repeated along the upper mainplane in between the
roundels. It is believed that J8084, was flown by the unit's CO, S/Ldr Raymond
Collishaw, (the famous WWI leader of 'Black Flight' 10 Naval Air Squadron), and
featured a Squadron Leader's pennant under the cockpit.

AW Siskin III, J7764, 41 Sqn, RAF Northolt, 1926
After reforming in 1923 at RAF Northolt, initially on Sopwith Snipes, in early 1924,
41 Squadron re-equipped with Siskin IIIs. J7764, which joined the squadron in the
summer, displays 41 Squadron's broad red bar only applied to the fuselage, forward
of the roundel, (which was later extended along the whole fuselage flanking the roundel
and terminating just beneath the leading edge of the tailplane. The red bar was applied to
the upper mainplane between the roundels. After serving with Duxford's Meteorological Flight
in 1927, J7764 was returned to the manufacturers and converted in to a tandem seat IIIDC,
and served with 3 FTS then 5 FTS from May 1929 to October 1931.

AW Siskin IIIA, J9901, 19 Sqn, RAF Duxford, circa 1930
In 1926, the improved Siskin IIIA, with the more powerful Jaguar IV engine which improved performance above 10,000ft, was introduced into RAF service. The Siskin IIIA's most obvious external difference was the revised fin and rudder that did away with the ventral fin strake. 19 Squadron received its first Siskin IIIAs in 1928, and it will be noted that all Siskins (both III and IIIA) carried roundels in a 1-2-3 ratio in all six positions, although being a sesquiplane, they were positioned under the top wing rather than under the lower one which simply featured the serial number. The hyphen between the letter and the first numeral of the serial was a feature common to all RAF Fighters at this time and it also appears that the rudder striping has been amended with Red leading. J9901 joined 19 Squadron on 14 March 1930 and carries the squadron's blue and white checks on the fuselage, again forward of the roundel only, and between the roundels on the upper wing.

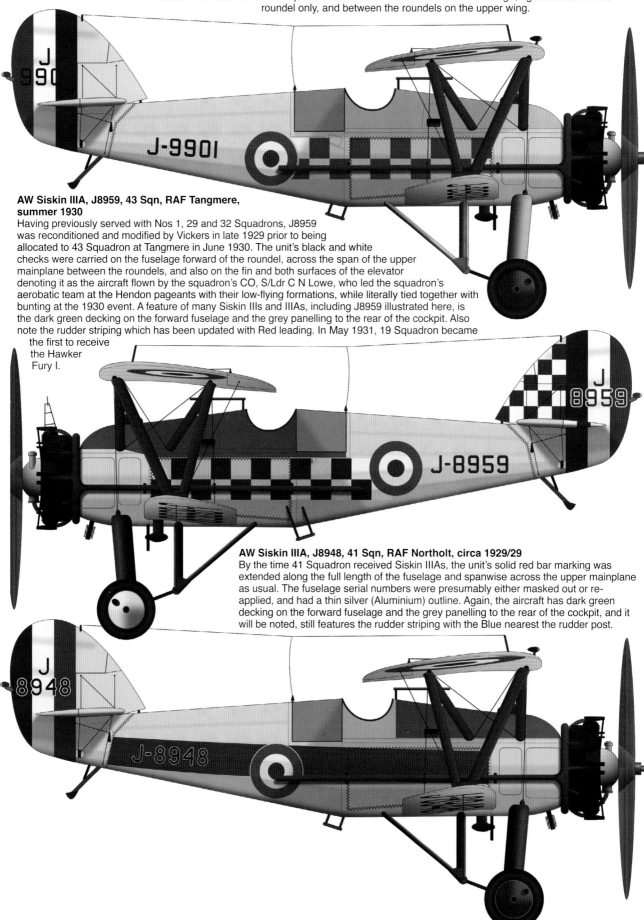

AW Siskin IIIA, J8959, 43 Sqn, RAF Tangmere, summer 1930
Having previously served with Nos 1, 29 and 32 Squadrons, J8959 was reconditioned and modified by Vickers in late 1929 prior to being allocated to 43 Squadron at Tangmere in June 1930. The unit's black and white checks were carried on the fuselage forward of the roundel, across the span of the upper mainplane between the roundels, and also on the fin and both surfaces of the elevator denoting it as the aircraft flown by the squadron's CO, S/Ldr C N Lowe, who led the squadron's aerobatic team at the Hendon pageants with their low-flying formations, while literally tied together with bunting at the 1930 event. A feature of many Siskin IIIs and IIIAs, including J8959 illustrated here, is the dark green decking on the forward fuselage and the grey panelling to the rear of the cockpit. Also note the rudder striping which has been updated with Red leading. In May 1931, 19 Squadron became the first to receive the Hawker Fury I.

AW Siskin IIIA, J8948, 41 Sqn, RAF Northolt, circa 1929/29
By the time 41 Squadron received Siskin IIIAs, the unit's solid red bar marking was extended along the full length of the fuselage and spanwise across the upper mainplane as usual. The fuselage serial numbers were presumably either masked out or re-applied, and had a thin silver (Aluminium) outline. Again, the aircraft has dark green decking on the forward fuselage and the grey panelling to the rear of the cockpit, and it will be noted, still features the rudder striping with the Blue nearest the rudder post.

Representative wing upper surface Squadron markings

No 19 Sqn (Siskin IIIA)

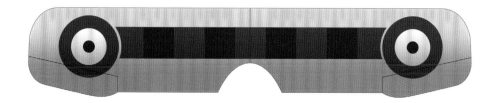

No 23 Sqn (Gamecock)

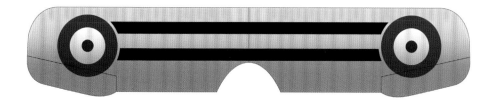

No 25 Sqn (Grebe)

No 29 Sqn (Grebe)

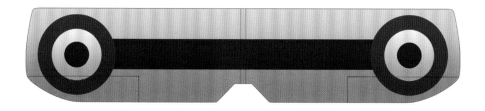

No 41 Sqn (Siskin IIIA)

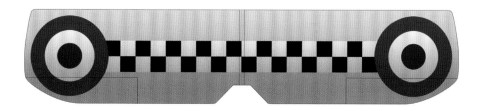

No 43 Sqn (Siskin IIIA)

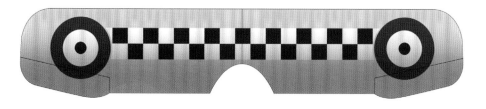

No 56 Sqn (Grebe)

Bristol Bulldog II, J9576, 3 Sqn, RAF Upavon, summer 1929
No. 3 Squadron reformed at RAF Manston (having previously briefly served in India post-war) initially on Sopwith Snipes, and then Hawker Woodcocks and Gloster Gamecocks, before receiving Bulldog IIs in May 1929. J9576 was received by 3 Squadron in June 1929 and carries the unit's emerald green bar along the full length of the fuselage, as well as the full span of the upper wing between the roundels. The fuselage spine was dark green, extending the full length of the fuselage and the rudder still has the Blue stripe leading. Also of interest are the red mainwheel hubs, possibly denoting A Flight, and the gloss black interplane and cabane struts, a common feature on Bulldog IIs.

Bristol Bulldog IIA, K1081, 17 Sqn, RAF Upavon, June 1930
No. 17 Squadron was the second squadron to re-equip with the Bulldog IIA when it exchanged its Siskin IIIAs for Bulldog II and IIAs in October 1929, inheriting some airframes from the co-located 3 Squadron, resulting for a time in a mix of unit markings! K1081 carried 3 Squadron's emerald green bar on its upper wing with 17 Squadron's black zig-zag marking along the full length of its fuselage sides. Again, the fuselage spine was dark green, extending the full length of the fuselage, the rudder still had the Blue stripe leading and the interplane and cabane struts were gloss black. K1081 collided with a Bulldog II on 6 May 1931 during a practice attack on a bomber formation and crashed.

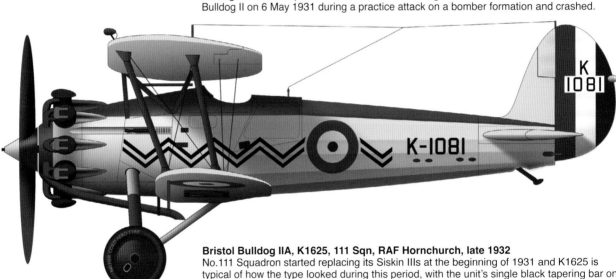

Bristol Bulldog IIA, K1625, 111 Sqn, RAF Hornchurch, late 1932
No.111 Squadron started replacing its Siskin IIIs at the beginning of 1931 and K1625 is typical of how the type looked during this period, with the unit's single black tapering bar on the fuselage, extending from just aft of the cockpit to the rudder hinge, obscuring the fuselage serials which only appeared on the rudder and under the lower mainplane. A black bar was applied to the upper mainplane between the roundels. Of interest is the lack of the dark green fuselage spine (which seems common during this period), and the rudder colours are now reversed with red leading.

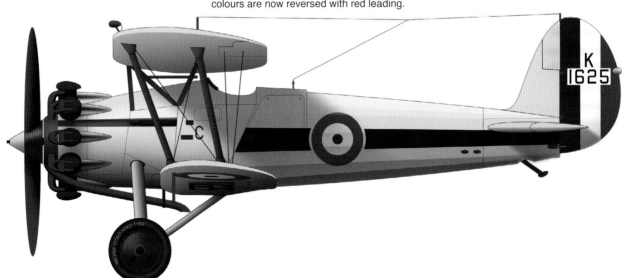

Bristol Bulldog IIA, K1606, 32 Sqn, RAF Biggin Hill, late 1934
K1606 was amongst the first Bulldog IIAs to enter service with 32 Squadron, in early
1931, and remained with unit until July 1936 when the type was replaced by Gloster
Gauntlet IIs and K1606 became instructional airframe 905M. Finished in the standard
overall Aluminium (silver) scheme, without the dark green fuselage spine, it will be
noticed that K1606 doesn't carry rudder striping either, following the issue of an AMO to
discontinue the practice in August 1934. K1606 also features some of the modifications
that were applied to surviving Mk.IIAs in 1933, including fitting a tailwheel in lieu of the
tailskid, Dunlop disc mainwheels, and an enlarged fin. The Squadron's markings
consisted of a blue fuselage band from cockpit to tailplane interrupted by two diagonal
(silver) gaps. The band on the upper mainplane surfaces having three diagonal gaps.
The black fuselage serial was outlined in Aluminium. The motif on the fin is that of Bristol
Aeroplane Company's 'Bulldog' logo.

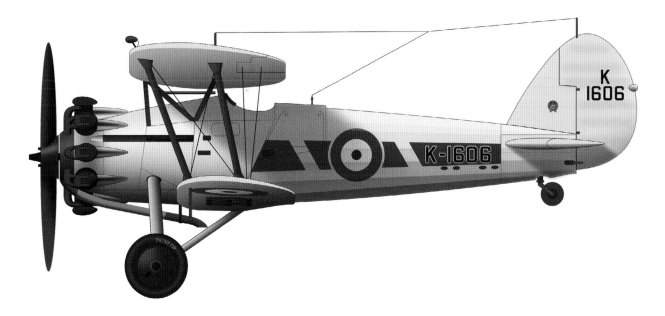

Representative wing upper surface Squadron markings

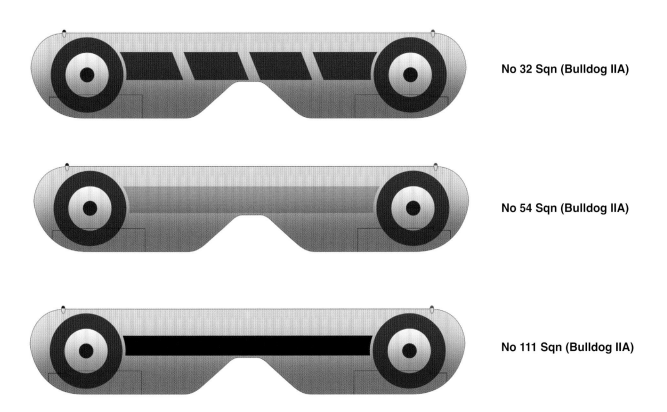

No 32 Sqn (Bulldog IIA)

No 54 Sqn (Bulldog IIA)

No 111 Sqn (Bulldog IIA)

Hawker Fury I, K2900, 1 Sqn, RAF Tangmere, 1934
K2900 was one of six Fury Is delivered at a time when rudder stripes were still being applied. Allocated to 1 Squadron on 28 May 1934 and coded 'K', K2900 served with the unit throughout its service life which ended in November 1937 in a crash landing at Tangmere. Finished in the overall 'silver' scheme, the brightly polished natural metal cowling panels contrasted sharply with the V84 Aluminium painted fabric areas. The squadron's parallel red bars tapered to a point aft of the fuselage roundel, leaving a gap for the serial number, but remained parallel across the upper mainplane (see opposite). All the national markings (rudder stripes and roundels) are in the Bright Red VR3 and Bright Blue VB2 shades, and the squadron bars and the individual aircraft letter 'K' in Bright Red. K2900's rudder stripes were probably removed in October 1935.

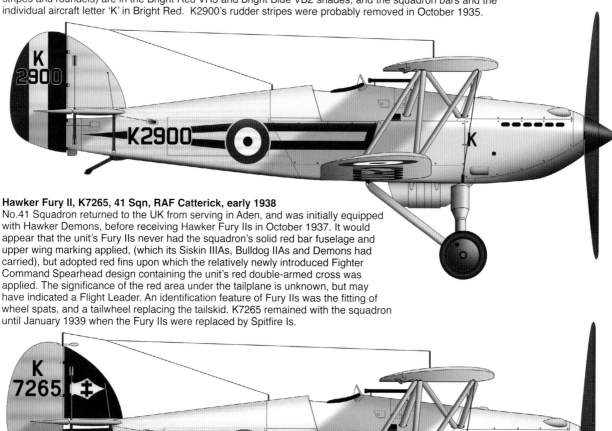

Hawker Fury II, K7265, 41 Sqn, RAF Catterick, early 1938
No.41 Squadron returned to the UK from serving in Aden, and was initially equipped with Hawker Demons, before receiving Hawker Fury IIs in October 1937. It would appear that the unit's Fury IIs never had the squadron's solid red bar fuselage and upper wing marking applied, (which its Siskin IIIAs, Bulldog IIAs and Demons had carried), but adopted red fins upon which the relatively newly introduced Fighter Command Spearhead design containing the unit's red double-armed cross was applied. The significance of the red area under the tailplane is unknown, but may have indicated a Flight Leader. An identification feature of Fury IIs was the fitting of wheel spats, and a tailwheel replacing the tailskid. K7265 remained with the squadron until January 1939 when the Fury IIs were replaced by Spitfire Is.

**Hawker Fury II, K8267, 8 Flying Training School,
RAF Montrose, Scotland, winter 1939**
Following frontline squadron service, Fury IIs, also saw use with Flying Training Schools. With wheel spats removed (to prevent clogging), Fury II, K8267 '7' from Montrose-based 8 FTS was re-finished in Dark Earth and Dark Green upper surfaces – upper and lower mainplanes, tailplane, fuselage, fin and top section of the rudder – with Yellow under surfaces and rear fuselage sides, although the forward section of the fuselage and nose remained in silver dope/natural metal. The serial number was re-applied in white on the rudder. 8 FTS was renamed 8 Service Flying Training School (SFTS) at outbreak of war on 3 September 1939 and disposed of its Fury IIs, K8267 becoming an instructional airframe on 17 January 1940. 8 SFTS was subsequently disbanded on 25 March 1942 and absorbed by 2 Flying Instructors School.

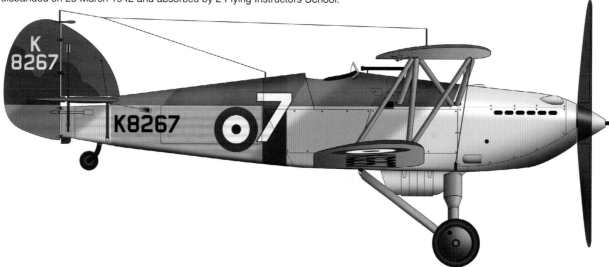

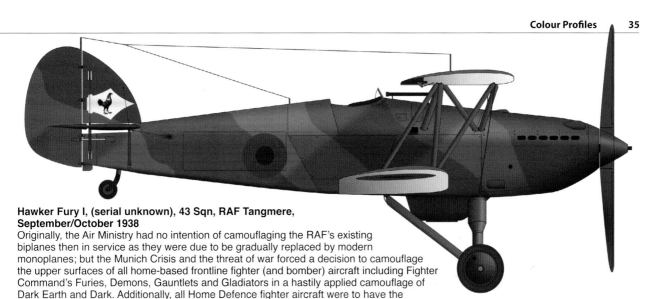

Hawker Fury I, (serial unknown), 43 Sqn, RAF Tangmere, September/October 1938
Originally, the Air Ministry had no intention of camouflaging the RAF's existing biplanes then in service as they were due to be gradually replaced by modern monoplanes; but the Munich Crisis and the threat of war forced a decision to camouflage the upper surfaces of all home-based frontline fighter (and bomber) aircraft including Fighter Command's Furies, Demons, Gauntlets and Gladiators in a hastily applied camouflage of Dark Earth and Dark. Additionally, all Home Defence fighter aircraft were to have the undersides of their wings and tailplanes painted Night (a very dark blue-grey shade) and White, to allow the Royal Observer Corps to track them and avoid them being shot at by anti-aircraft gunners. The under surface of the port wing was to be finished in Night and the under surface of the starboard wing in White, the division between the colours running down the centreline of the aircraft. Additionally the roundels were toned down, those on the wing upper surfaces and fuselage sides by overpainting the White areas in Red and Blue, in the VNR5 and VNB6 'dull' shades. Serial numbers were also (initially) overpainted, although some squadrons retained their unit identity by keeping the Fighter spearhead on the fin, in this case containing 43 Squadron's gamecock motif.

At this time no Air Diagram camouflage patterns had been designed for biplanes, so all the aircraft were painted in Dark Earth and Dark Green upper surfaces to whatever patterns were deemed suitable, many being based upon simplified versions of the new Air Diagrams for single-engined monoplanes such as AD 1158 and AD 1160.

The Air Ministry also concluded that there was no legal reason why roundels on the underside of Home Defence fighter aircraft were necessary, as the Night and White finish would act as sufficient identification from below, but some squadrons (like 43 Squadron) merely toned the existing roundels down by overpainting them in Red and Blue like the upper wing and fuselage sides. Initially underwing serial numbers were to remain – in White under the (Night) port wing and Night under the (White) starboard, although this order was soon amended and underwing serials were painted over on all types except training aircraft.

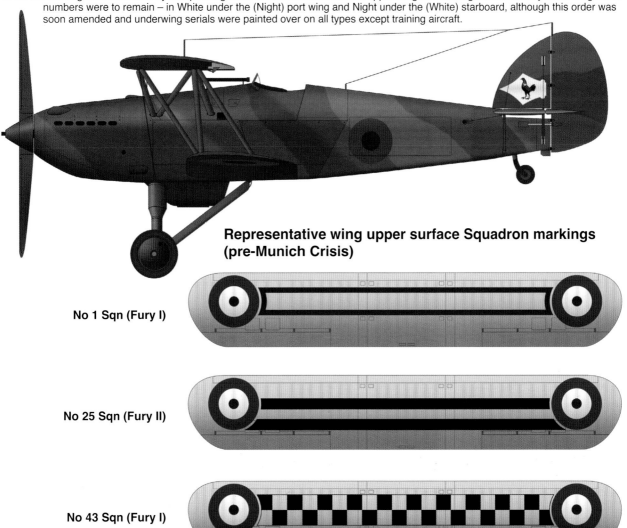

Representative wing upper surface Squadron markings (pre-Munich Crisis)

No 1 Sqn (Fury I)

No 25 Sqn (Fury II)

No 43 Sqn (Fury I)

Hawker Demon, K2850 'L', 23 Sqn, RAF Biggin Hill, May 1933
Resplendent in the squadron's red and blue markings which ran from the cockpit to the leading
edge of the tailplane on the fuselage, and between the roundels on the upper wing, it will be
noticed that the fuselage serial number was painted around leaving it on a 'silver' rectangle. The
squadron's badge, a red eagle preying on a yellow falcon, was carried on the fin and the aircraft's
individual code letter 'L' was applied on the nose under the exhaust manifold. And the mainwheel
hubs were red, possibly indicating A Flight. K2850 served with 23 Squadron from May 1933 to
August 1935 after which it was sent to Malta to join 74 Squadron. Following its return to Britain,
K2850 went on to serve with 41 and 64 Squadrons prior to joining 600 Squadron in February 1938
and was finally SOC on 29 May 1940.

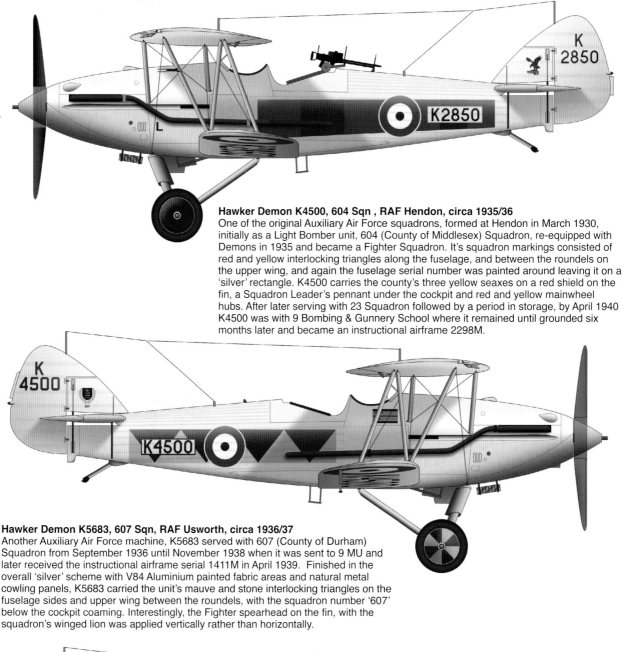

Hawker Demon K4500, 604 Sqn , RAF Hendon, circa 1935/36
One of the original Auxiliary Air Force squadrons, formed at Hendon in March 1930,
initially as a Light Bomber unit, 604 (County of Middlesex) Squadron, re-equipped with
Demons in 1935 and became a Fighter Squadron. It's squadron markings consisted of
red and yellow interlocking triangles along the fuselage, and between the roundels on
the upper wing, and again the fuselage serial number was painted around leaving it on a
'silver' rectangle. K4500 carries the county's three yellow seaxes on a red shield on the
fin, a Squadron Leader's pennant under the cockpit and red and yellow mainwheel
hubs. After later serving with 23 Squadron followed by a period in storage, by April 1940
K4500 was with 9 Bombing & Gunnery School where it remained until grounded six
months later and became an instructional airframe 2298M.

Hawker Demon K5683, 607 Sqn, RAF Usworth, circa 1936/37
Another Auxiliary Air Force machine, K5683 served with 607 (County of Durham)
Squadron from September 1936 until November 1938 when it was sent to 9 MU and
later received the instructional airframe serial 1411M in April 1939. Finished in the
overall 'silver' scheme with V84 Aluminium painted fabric areas and natural metal
cowling panels, K5683 carried the unit's mauve and stone interlocking triangles on the
fuselage sides and upper wing between the roundels, with the squadron number '607'
below the cockpit coaming. Interestingly, the Fighter spearhead on the fin, with the
squadron's winged lion was applied vertically rather than horizontally.

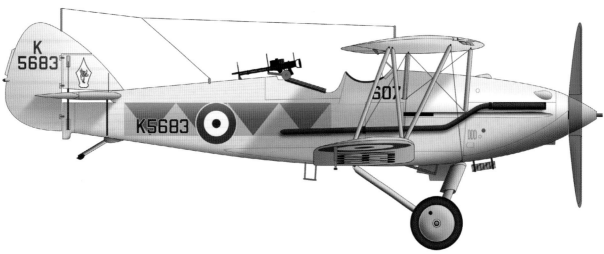

Representative wing upper surface Squadron markings (pre-Munich Crisis)

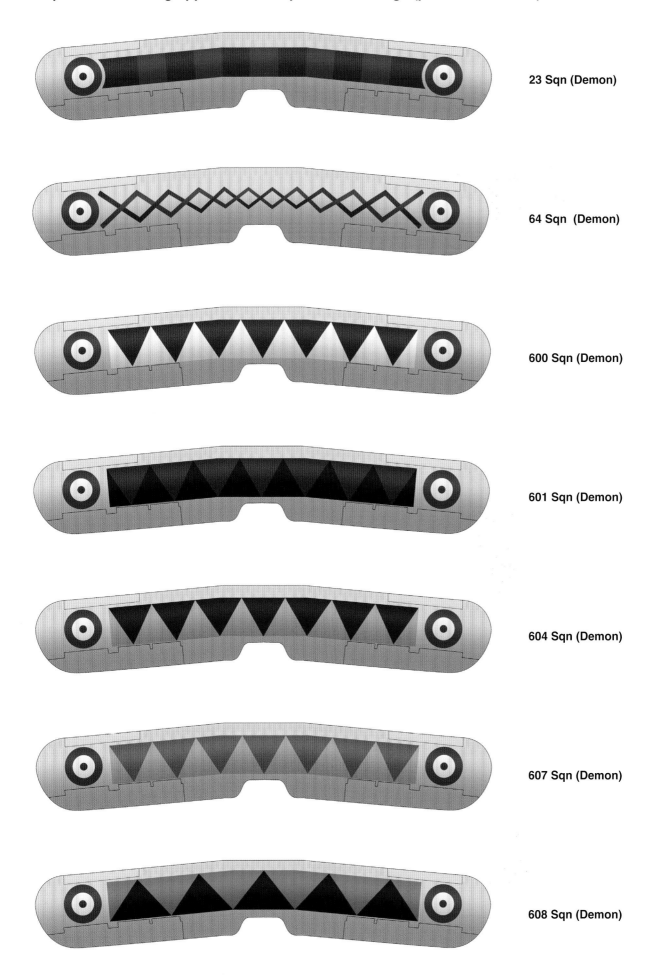

23 Sqn (Demon)

64 Sqn (Demon)

600 Sqn (Demon)

601 Sqn (Demon)

604 Sqn (Demon)

607 Sqn (Demon)

608 Sqn (Demon)

Hawker Demon K3767 or K3769, 74 Sqn, Hal Far, Malta, circa 1935
Re-formed in September 1935, at Hal Far, Malta, at the start of the so-called Abyssinian Crisis when Italy invaded Abyssinia, East Africa, 74 Squadron was charged with conducting a series of camouflage trials to investigate methods of reducing the visibility of aircraft when viewed from above. A variety of colours were used, and K3767 (or K3769, the last number of this aircraft's serial is tantalisingly hidden under a patch of dark paint), is thought to have been painted in Dark Earth and Dark Green upper surfaces, while retaining the 'silver' doped under sides.

Hawker Demon, K5698, 'MS-G', 23 Sqn, RAF Wittering, autumn 1938
Fitted with a Nash & Thompson power operated gun turret, K5698 was camouflaged, probably in Dark Earth and Dark Green upper surfaces (as illustrated) with Night/White under surfaces. Still retaining its Red/White/Blue fuselage roundels its upperwing roundels were probably painted over.   Following the introduction of squadron code letters during the Munich Crisis, 23 Squadron was allocated 'MS' and K5698 the individual aircraft letter 'G', both applied in Medium Sea Grey. The serial number was painted out on both the fuselage sides and under the wings, although the 'last two' of the serial '98' was roughly applied (in chalk or paint) on the rudder. Also of note is the black cowling front which extended diagonally forwards and downwards from the front cockpit coaming. K5898 went on to serve with 9 BGS (Bombing & Gunnery School) and 24 EFTS (Elementary Flying Training School) before becoming Instructional Airframe 2326M in November 1940.

Hawker Demon TT, K2857, Royal Aircraft Establishment, Farnborough, Hampshire, late 1938/early 1939
Having briefly served with 23 Squadron in the summer of 1935, K2857 was assigned to the RAE where presumably at some point there, it was given this colour scheme of overall Yellow with black diagonal bands of varying widths. Converted in to target-tug (TT) configuration, the rectangular container designed to hold a towed target prior to it being deployed is just visible below the fuselage. It is thought that K2857 (and K2856) were used by the RAE to test and trial the installation,

Hawker Demon (serial unknown), 74 Sqn, Hal Far, Malta, circa 1935
Quantities of camouflage paint developed by the Royal Aircraft Establishment (RAE) were sent to Malta to be applied on various aircraft types, including 74 Squadron's Demons, in a variety of camouflage patterns for a series of camouflage trials conducted by the Air Ministry. It is difficult to accurately determine what this particular aircraft's colour scheme was (serial overpainted), but Dark Earth, Dark Green, Light Earth, Light Green and Dark Sea Grey were amongst the RAE paint samples sent to Malta for use on a proposed 'Land Plane Scheme'. At least two of the RAE colours were additionally 'modified' – by adding red dope to Dark Earth to make a dark red-brown called 'Malta Soil' and white dope to Light Earth to make a beige shade referred to as 'Malta Rock'. The fuselage and wing upper surface Red/White/Blue roundels were overpainted and just one re-applied, in the 'lo-viz' Red/Blue style (in the Dull shades), in various positions on the upper wing.

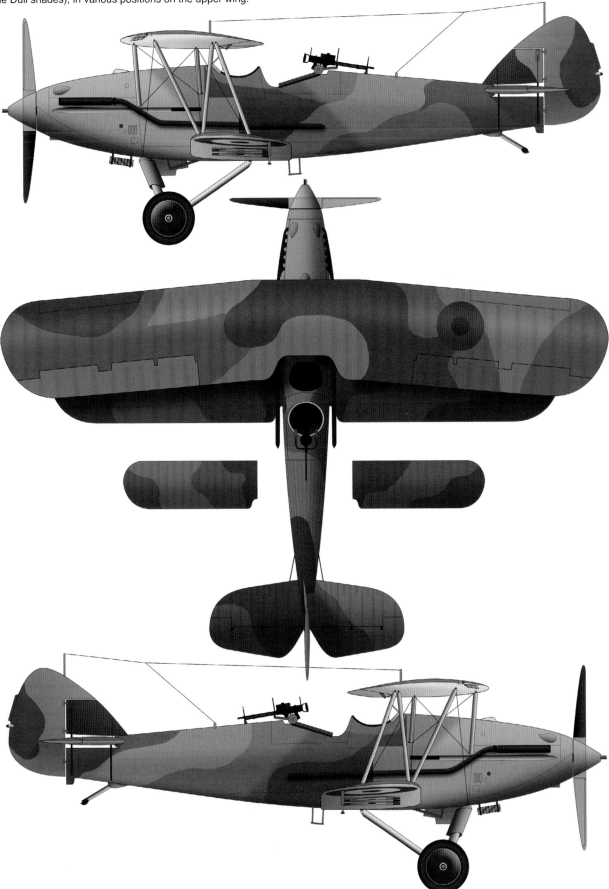

Continued from page 27

87 Squadron at Tangmere both received the Fury II in March 1937, whereas Catterick-based 41 Squadron received its allocation a few months later in October. While both 73 and 87 Squadrons would re-equip with the Gladiator I in June or July 1937, 41 Squadron was destined to soldier on with its Furies until January 1939, as indeed did 43 Squadron which was still using the Fury I and is believed to have been the last operational squadron to finally surrender their Furies – by a slender margin.

Left:

The Munich Crisis of September 1938 and its attendant threat of war resulted in all home-based frontline fighter (and bomber aircraft) being hastily camouflaged using drab tones in whatever patterns were thought suitable. The sombre effect was further emphasised by the toning down of all roundels or, temporarily at least, their disappearance from upper wing surfaces entirely. This image of 43 Squadron's Fury Is, seen in late-September or October 1938, demonstrates the point, given that not only have their wing roundels been obscured, but so to have their serial numbers. In fact, the only clue as to this unit's identity is the fighter spearhead on the fin containing 43 Squadron's gamecock motif on ten of the twelve aircraft. *Courtesy of Andy Thomas*

Below:

43 Squadron Fury Is fitted with tailwheels in lieu of their original tail skids. Seemingly only Mk.IIs were fitted with tailwheels but as later images show, some Mk.IIs received skids initially. Thus, the presence of a tailwheel was not a foolproof method of determining a Fury's Mark.. *Courtesy of Andy Thomas*

Many Furies, perhaps 140, served with no less than nine flying training schools, the CFS, RAF College (RAFC), 1 Air Armament School (AAS) and 2 Anti-Aircraft Co-operation Unit (AACU) from 1933 onwards to provide advanced flying training and weapons training for pilots due to be posted to operational units. The last airworthy RAF Furies were grounded in 1940.

Hawker Fury I production batches:
21 x Mk.I del 4.31
(K1926 - K1946)
48 x Mk.I del 1.32 to 4.32
(K2035 - K2082)
10 x Mk.I del 12.32 and 1.33
(K2874 - K2883)
6 x Mk.I del 1.33
(K2899 - K2904)
13 x Mk.I del 9.32 to 11.32
(K3730 - K3742)
20 x Mk.I del 11.35 to 12.35
(K5663 - K5682)

Hawker Fury II production batches:
23 x Mk.II del 10.36 to 12.36
(K7263 - K7285)

89 x Mk.II del 7.36 to 4.37
(K8218 - K8306) all built by General Aircraft Ltd

Notes.
1) Twenty-two Fury Is were sent to the SAAF between late-June and October 1940 to supplement seven examples bought before the war. Although no Fury II was ever supplied from RAF stocks, the original SAAF Furies were all fitted with the Kestrel VI as used by the Fury II, which in turn might have given rise to a belief that ex-RAF Fury IIs were supplied to the SAAF.

2) Of the twenty-three Fury IIs in batch K7263 to K7285, all but the last two (K7284 and K7285) went to 25 Squadron. Of the second and largest batch twenty-five went directly to FTS units, seven went directly to the CFS, three to the RAFC and one to the AAS. The remaining fifty-three were sent to aircraft storage units from where most went to training units with only a relative few being allocated to operational squadrons.

Top left:
Wearing Trainer Yellow and polished metal finish, Fury I K5670 was delivered to 2 ASU in November 1935. Later allocated to 7 FTS, it was serving with 5 FTS by late 1938 coded '3'. Renamed 5 Service Flying Training School (SFTS) on 3 September 1939 with an establishment of thirty-one Harts and forty-two Airspeed Oxfords, it seems that the Furies had become surplus to requirements and disposed of with K5670 being delivered to 5 MU by 16 January 1940. This was not quite the end for K5670 however, as it was transferred to the SAAF in June 1940 becoming 208.

Bottom left:
Briefly operated by 43 Squadron for service trials, K3586 never formally entered RAF service. Built privately as a Fury I variant, it first flew on 3 May 1933 and was known as the Hawker High Speed Fury. Used as a testbed for a variety of Kestrel and Rolls-Royce Goshawk engines, K3586 was also used to trial airframe variations including experiments with swept-back upper and swept-forward lower wings, various wing struts and a variety of wheel spats – achieving, in one of its many forms, the astonishing (in 1933) maximum level speed of 258 mph. Although the High Speed Fury itself never gained a production order, the numerous trials carried out did lead to the development of the Fury II, thus justifying K3586's inclusion here. When photographed K3586 was fitted with the ultimately unsuccessful Goshawk steam-cooled engine with steam-condensers fitted along the length of the top wing which did away with the need for drag-inducing radiators. K3586 was written off on 29 August 1933 when the undercarriage collapsed on landing.

Left:
Immaculate echelon starboard formation of nine 25 Squadron Fury IIs, this Mark being readily identified from the Fury I by their mainwheel spats – until they were removed of course. The aircraft seen here are from the first production batch delivered between October and December 1936, the majority of which were initially issued to 25 Squadron before they were passed to 41 Squadron in October 1937 when 25 Squadron became a Demon equipped night-fighter unit. Carrying 25 Squadron's black parallel bar markings on the fuselage sides and upper wing, these aircraft also feature fighter spearheads on their fins with the squadron motif set within. The squadron leader's aircraft, K7270 in the foreground, and the Flight Leaders' aircraft, K7271 and K7274, have 'solid' colour fins and tailplanes (black for K7270 and we assume red and blue for the Flight Leaders) whereas the others display the spearhead within forward-facing chevrons, presumably also in Flight colours.

Below:
Seen while serving with 41 Squadron in 1938, Fury II, K7265, was one of those involved in an unusual exchange of aircraft in October 1937 whereby 25 Squadron received 41 Squadron's Demons. Unlike so many fighter units prior to Munich, 41 Squadron didn't apply any specific markings to the fuselage or upper wings, instead they contented themselves with red fins and a white fighter spearhead containing the unit's red double-armed cross which originated from their association with St Omer, France, in 1916 – the location of the unit's first overseas base. The cross, part of the town's coat of arms, was approved by King George VI in February 1937. Photographed in its prime, complete with wheel spats and tailwheel, K7265 appears to have remained with the squadron until January 1939 when the Furies were replaced by Spitfire Is. Subsequently stored at 5 MU, K7265 became instructional airframe 2033M in June 1940.

Bottom:
With wheel spats removed to prevent clogging, Fury II, K8267 '7', K8261 '4' and K8262 '3' from Montrose-based 8 FTS formate above a wintery landscape in 1939. All three were delivered to 1 ASU in December 1936 prior to being delivered to 8 FTS the following year. 8 FTS was renamed 8 SFTS on 3 September 1939 and disposed of its Furies. All three of those seen here became instructional airframes on 17 January 1940.

Hawker Demon I, turreted Demon and Turret Demon

When the Hawker Hart light bomber entered RAF service in 1930, its speed, manoeuvrability and rate of climb was such that contemporary fighters, unless precisely positioned, faced real difficulties intercepting it. The Hart represented success for the manufacturer and a challenge to air forces. Its basic design would, given appropriate modifications, help answer the Exchequer's plea for economy and the RAF's requirement for an improved light bomber (Hind), new army co-operation aircraft (Audax and Hector), a new general purpose type (Hardy), and an advanced trainer which became the Hart Trainer.

In addition, a perceived requirement arose for a Hart-based two-seat fighter that would later emerge as the Demon, the first examples of which were known as the Hart Fighter. Fitted with a more powerful version of the Kestrel than that used by Hart bombers they were armed with two fixed forward-firing Vickers guns as opposed to one, while the gunner was equipped with the ubiquitous Lewis gun in a modified rear cockpit featuring a cut-down coaming on either beam to improve its arc of fire.

Six Hart Fighters were procured, all going to Bulldog-equipped 23 Squadron in July 1931 where they formed a separate flight and soon proved they could match the Bulldog's manoeuvrability while

Top right:
Demon K4518 seen while temporarily attached to D Flight of 6 Squadron at Ismailia, Egypt, in 1936 without any hint of a unit marking. Due to a general threat to British interests in the eastern Mediterranean, Palestine and Abyssinia during 1935/36, Demons were sent from Britain to these locations to provide an element of air defence. Thus 6 Squadron, a Hart-equipped army co-operation unit, temporarily added 'D' Flight's fighters to its establishment from October 1935 to late 1936. Based near Suez some of its aircraft were forward based to Ramleh, Palestine. Returning to the UK, K4518 was issued to 64 Squadron on 1 November 1937, but stalled and crashed at the end of the month.

Bottom right:
Illustrating the effectiveness of the experimental camouflage colours being trialled, this formation of five 74 Squadron Demons, seen over Hal Far, show the variations in camouflage patterns as well as the different colours used. Sadly, it is difficult to determine what the precise colours were. Of equal interest is the unusual positioning of the single upper wing red/blue roundels applied in the dull VNR5 and VNB6 shades. Under surfaces retained their original V84 Aluminium finish with the original 1-3-5 ratio VR3 Bright Red, VW3 White and VB2 Bright Blue underwing roundels and black serial numbers. Visible on the starboard upper wing of the Demon situated on the right of the 'vic' leader is the square outline of a Youngman dinghy-type floatation gear recess which was included on replacement starboard upper mainplanes sent to Malta to replace existing wings. *Tony O'Toole collection*

Above:
Revealing a hint of a partial serial number on its rudder, this 74 Squadron Demon is either K3767 or K3769 and was photographed at Hal Far, Malta, during the 1935 Abyssinian Crisis (Mussolini's invasion of Abyssinia) where the unit's aircraft were included in a series of camouflage trials. The trials, conducted by the Air Ministry and RAE, investigated methods of reducing the visibility of aircraft when viewed from above whether on the ground or in flight. Quantities of camouflage paint developed by the RAE were sent to Malta to be employed on various aircraft types, including 74 Squadron's Demons, and applied using a variety of prescribed camouflage patterns. It is difficult to accurately determine what this particular aircraft's colour scheme was, but Dark Earth, Dark Green, Light Earth, Light Green, Dark Sea Grey and possibly another grey colour were amongst the RAE paint samples sent to Malta for use on a Land Plane Scheme. To further confuse matters, at least two of the RAE colours were 'modified' – one by adding red dope to Dark Earth to make a dark red-brown called 'Malta Soil' and white dope to Light Earth to make a beige shade referred to as 'Malta Rock'. Note the solitary red/blue roundel (in the duller 'night' shades) on the starboard upper wing tip. *Tony O'Toole collection*

Top left:
A 74 Squadron Demon seen at Hal Far displaying a further variation of the experimental camouflage pattern scheme.

possessing a significant advantage in terms of speed and rate of climb. Consequently, seventeen production examples were ordered with most going to 23 Squadron from July 1933, enabling the unit to dispense with Bulldogs entirely. The new fighter had earlier been christened 'Demon' in July 1932,

The Demon reintroduced the two-seat, single-engine day fighter to RAF service, a concept made famous years earlier by the Bristol F.2B Fighter in particular, although it was soon discovered that the much greater speed of the Demon (181 mph at 13,400ft) made it hard for the gunner to train his weapon at higher speeds – anything over 130 mph. An answer to the problem was sought.

Centre:
As indicated by the number below the cockpit, Demon K5683 belonged to 607 Squadron who operated the type from September 1936 until April 1939 although the unit's last example lingered until August, months after they received their first Gladiator in December 1938. Prior to Munich, 607's colours consisted of mauve and stone interlocking triangles on the fuselage and upper wing between the roundels. Unusually, because the fighter spearhead on the fin encompasses a vertical winged lion motif, the spearhead itself is placed vertically rather than horizontally. Formed in 1930 as a day bomber unit flying the Westland Wapiti IIA, by late 1936 the unit had been repurposed as a Demon-equipped fighter squadron. Delivered to 607 Squadron on 18 September 1936, K5683 remained until November 1938 when it went to 9 MU.

Bottom left:
Delivered new to 601 Squadron in April 1937, Demon K5722 survived until 8 January 1938 when it crashed at Upavon, although its remains were not finally struck off charge for many months thereafter. The squadron colours consisted of interlocking red and black triangles on the fuselage and upper wing, examples of which are discernible on K5721 to the left. A pair of Gladiators can be seen behind K5722.

Right:
J9933 (the first production Hart and later the prototype Demon) was used in numerous tests and trials during its service life, several being devoted to finding ways of protecting Demon rear gunners from the type's slipstream; gunners having experienced significant difficulty in aiming their gun at speeds over 130 mph. The FN1 turret (seen here) was fitted to J9933 either in late 1933 or early 1934 and did assist gunners to improve their accuracy, albeit at a cost to the pilots who found that when rotated the FN1 disturbed the Demon's trim sufficiently to upset the pilot's aim when sighting his guns.

Bottom:
Three Boulton Paul-built 29 Squadron Demons seen in 1937 or 1938 after their return to the UK following the Abyssinian crisis. Bereft of their traditional 'XXX' fighter markings worn by their Demons in 1935, the leading Demon, K5737, nevertheless displays a fighter spearhead on its fin encompassing the unit motif – an eagle in flight preying on a buzzard. This image also illustrates the reduced diameter upperwing roundels introduced from August 1934 which didn't overlap the ailerons. All three are fitted with FN1 turrets of which K5900 was a Turret Demon (equipped with such from the outset) while the other two, K5736 and K5737, were turreted Demons, their FN1's being installed retrospectively. By 1 November 1939 K5900 (nearest) was serving with 1 AAS which operated a fleet of fifteen Demons amongst a host of other types, but by 2 January 1941 it had become 2460M. K5736 (furthest) ultimately served with 3 B&GS from late 1939 until, on 24 February 1940, it collided with another Demon and crashed near Donna Nook. After serving with 29 Squadron, followed by time in storage, K5737's last posting was to 9 B&GS on 3 April 1940 where it survived to become 2290M in October that year.

Left:
A familiar image of the Frazer-Nash 'Lobster-back' turret armed with a .303in Mk.III Lewis machine gun for which six 97-round ammunition drums were carried. As can be seen the gunner was protected by a four-segment semi-enclosed shield. J9933 was later designated instructional airframe 1120M and allocated to 2 SoTT in September 1938.

Ultimately a solution was achieved with the development of a 'lobster-back' hydraulic turret, the FN1, produced by Nash & Thompson.* The FN1 was trialled initially in the first production Hart J9933 in late 1933 or 1934, it being found that the turret did assist gunners to improve their accuracy, albeit at a cost to the pilot whose aim was disrupted when the turret rotated and upset the Demon's trim!

Procuring the Demon created ill-starred long-term consequences. Its introduction was inspired by a combination of factors: first, there was the legacy of the Bristol Fighter's success in WWI; second, economy – the Demon as a development of the existing Hart would be cheaper to buy; third, although we may presume that it was never his intention, Sydney Camm's quip about 'setting a Hart to catch a Hart' was apparently taken literally. Given the Demon's minimal performance advantage over the Hart the effective answer to intercepting it, or *any* bomber, in the early 1930s would have been the acquisition of the individually more expensive Hawker Fury. Unfortunately, the Demon's existence

Right:
A rare view showing the underside of 29 Squadron turreted Demon K5737. Photographed in 1937/38, the black rectangles partially obscuring the serial numbers are light bomb carriers.

would allow the concept of the single-engined two-seat fighter to be seen as an essential part of the RAF's day-fighter armoury: it wasn't. By September 1938, the need to replace the Demon had been long understood, but with eight squadrons still using it, it seems the RAF fell into the belief that they required a monoplane equivalent: they didn't.

Rather than pour resources into increasing single-seat day fighter production of the Hurricane, additional time and effort was lost in procuring the complex Boulton Paul Defiant. The latter, powered by a Rolls-Royce Merlin was, unlike the F.2B, devoid of fixed forward firing weapons and instead a second crewman operated a four-gun turret situated behind the pilot. True, the Defiant was promulgated as a bomber destroyer, but even before the type was selected for production lessons emerging from the Spanish Civil War were already casting doubts on the validity of this concept in the face of modern monoplane fighters. Despite a few early Battle of Britain successes, the Defiant was indeed proven to be tactically and technically misguided, defects the airmen who flew it into battle could not compensate for despite their gallantry!

In considering the Demon, the pilot did at least benefit by having two fixed forward-firing guns, weapons he would have used offensively while his gunner defended their rear, whereas the Defiant pilot had to solve the equation of how best to position his aircraft to allow the gunner to obtain a target while he made complex manoeuvres and maintained a lookout for intercepting enemy fighters. Airmen had discovered the flaw in these tactics over twenty-two years earlier.

The single-engined turret fighter represented a blind alley in British fighter design not just for the RAF, but for the Royal Navy's egregious Blackburn Roc turret fighter also. For the record, it is

important to understand that the Roc was born of an entirely different concept to the one that created the Defiant. Admiralty thinking centred upon a perceived need to obtain a carrier-borne fighter that could escort Swordfish torpedo bombers to and from their target, for which the turret-armed Roc seemed, in theory at least, to offer a reasonable solution. Given the low speed of even an unarmed Swordfish, the Roc's cruising speed of about 135 mph (maximum speed 220 mph) seemed adequate at the time for the role envisaged.

* *Esmonde Thompson and Archibald Frazer-Nash had established a company in 1929 called 'Nash & Thompson'. They developed hydraulic gun turrets invented by Frazer-Nash and marketed them using*

Above:
Photographed around the time of the Munich Crisis, this otherwise anonymous Demon, thought to be from 604 Squadron, has been partly camouflaged using Dark Earth and Dark Green, while the wings retain their original Aluminium finish and the forward fuselage remains, for the time being at least, brightly polished natural metal. The 'toned-down' fuselage roundel is now devoid of the colour white. *Andy Thomas*

Left:
K5698, a turreted Demon, was delivered to 23 Squadron pre-Munich and allocated the individual code letter 'G'. This image dates from between September and December 1938 by which time the airframe had received a three or four-colour disruptive pattern camouflage scheme – excluding the black painted cowling which extends diagonally forwards and downwards from the front cockpit coaming. As was common at this time, airframe serial numbers were painted out resulting, in this instance, with the last two digits being crudely applied on the rudder. The unit code 'MS' was allocated to 23 Squadron in September 1938 and was subsequently applied to Blenheim If fighters when they replaced the biplanes in December 1938. K5898 went on to serve with 9 BGS and 24 EFTS before becoming 2326M in November 1940. *Andy Thomas*

Above:
Having started life as a bomber unit flying the Wapiti IIA, a change of role took effect on 16 January 1937 when 608 Squadron became a Demon-equipped fighter squadron. Although this Demon remains unidentified, the photo itself dates from between October 1938 and March 1939; the squadron code 'PG' having been allocated in October 1938. This Demon carries the individual code 'P'. 608 Squadron retained the Demon in the fighter role until March 1939 when a further change resulted in 608 becoming a general reconnaissance unit equipped with the Avro Anson I.

Centre right:
Delivered new to 2 ASU in March 1933, Demon K2857 was assigned to the RAE in July where, except for a brief period with 23 Squadron in September 1935, it remained until March 1940 when it became instructional airframe 1853M. By far the most interesting aspect of this image is K2857's colour scheme – overall yellow with black bands of differing widths denoting a target-towing role or, more simply, a target-tug (TT). Visible below the fuselage is a rectangular container designed to hold a towed target prior to it being deployed. Presumably K2857 (and sister K2856) were used by the RAE towards the end of their service lives to test and trial the installation.

the soon-to-be familiar prefix 'FN'.

Sources differ as to how many Demons were built for the RAF. Hart Fighters included, it appears that 238 Demons were delivered to the RAF, with 126 being built and delivered by Hawker between 1933 and 1936, of which the last 49 received turrets at some stage. In addition, Boulton Paul delivered 106 Demons between September 1936 and early 1938, of which thirty-four were delivered as Turret Demons with twenty-eight others having turrets fitted retrospectively to thus become technically (and pedantically) turreted Demons.

**Hawker Demon
production batches:**
6 x Hawker Hart Fighters delivered 7.31
(**K1950 - K1955**)

Hawker-built Demons:
17 x Demon I del 2.33 to 3.33
(**K2842 - K2858**)
4 x Demon I del 3.33 (**K2905 - K2908**)
44 x Demon I del 6.34 to 8.34
(**K3764 - K3807**)
12 x Demon I del 8.34 to 9.34
(**K3974 - K3985**)
49 x turreted Demons del 5.35 to 2.36
(**K4496 - K4544**). Some delivered with turrets, others fitted when available

**Demons delivered by
Boulton Paul Wolverhampton:**
59 x Demon I del 9.36 to 7.37 (**K5683 - K5741**), of which 28 were later fitted with turrets to become turreted Demons
10 x Turret Demons del 7.37 and 8.37
(**K5898 -K5907**)
37 x Demon I del 9.37 to 1.38 (**K8181 - K8217**), of which K8181 to K8189, K8194 to K8204, K8214 to K8217 were delivered as Turret Demons

Above:
Permanently grounded, these unidentified wingless Demons (photographed in 1939 or 1940) were being used as instructional airframes for the training of groundcrew who were required by the RAF in previously undreamt of numbers. Hundreds of obsolete airframes would thus receive a second or even third lease of life, albeit an unsung one. Of the airframes seen here none are identifiable although the code 'WQ-O' seen on the nearest machine indicates that it once belonged to 604 Squadron.

Gloster Gauntlet I and II

The familiar two-bay, two-gun, open cockpit fighter, so familiar to RFC/RAF pilots since World War I found its last expression (with the RAF at least) with the acceptance into service of the Gloster Gauntlet. Thereafter, the type's successors would rapidly introduce a steady progression of new technologies, best demonstrated perhaps by the fact that while 19 Squadron introduced the Gauntlet into the RAF from January 1935, within a little over three years the same unit would introduce Spitfires into service.

The Gauntlet I was followed by increased quantities of the Gauntlet II, a

Below:
Gauntlet IIs initially entered service with 56 and 111 Squadrons in May and June 1936 respectively. Both these Gauntlet IIs wear 111 Squadron markings consisting of a solid black bar on the rear fuselage and upper mainplanes. K5269 is the CO's machine, namely S/Ldr G V Howard, DFC, as identified by the black cowling, fin and tailplanes plus the black triangle above the upper wing centre section. K5272 could be a flight commander's machine, possibly A Flight, with a red cowling, fin and tailplanes. Delivered to 111 Squadron in March 1936, K5269 crashed and was SOC on 23 March 1939, while K5272 was written off on 13 July 1938 following a landing accident when serving with 46 Squadron. The device in the centre of K5269's fin is thought to be the squadron badge in a standard frame.

Above:
The first Gauntlet I to enter RAF service was K4082 which was received by 19 Squadron on 25 January 1935. The last Mk.I to be delivered to the unit was K4097 which arrived on 8 June; in total 19 Squadron received nineteen of the twenty-four Mk.Is built. Three years later, in August 1938, the unit became the first to introduce the Spitfire into RAF service. The squadron's last Gauntlets left on 17 January 1939 although several Mk.Is were subsequently despatched to 6 Squadron in the Middle East to augment their existing Hawker Hardys. Here, K4092 reveals 19 Squadron's blue and white check markings along the fuselage sides and upper wing as well as its reduced diameter 35in upper wing roundels. This image dates from between 4 March 1935 (the date K4092 joined the unit), and 8 November 1935 when it was damaged beyond repair *DBR*.

Left:
Delivered to 54 Squadron in June 1936, Gauntlet II K5308 wears the unit's red and white diagonally-striped fuselage bar which also obscures the fuselage serial number – repeated, take our word for it, on the rudder. Whether the unit applied stripes to their upper wings is less certain. Previously, while equipped with the Bulldog IIA, the unit had used a solid yellow bar as their marking which was later altered to the one seen here. Subsequently allocated to 80 and then 74 Squadron, K5038 became 1557M in June 1939 and survived until finally SOC as late as 10 September 1945.

reflection of the growing concern
surrounding German rearmament.
Following the 1934 order for twenty-four
Mk.Is the next order, placed in April 1935,
was for 104 Gauntlet IIs to be delivered
between March and August 1936, an
order soon augmented by another for 100
Mk.IIs to be delivered between September
1936 and February 1937. While the
Gauntlet II was externally identical to the
Mk I the former was built using Hawker's
construction methods (including bolted
and riveted steel tube and duralumin
framework) following Hawker's takeover of
Gloster in 1934. This method was
considered to be much easier to build and
repair than Gloster's original welded
structure.

Both Marks proved capable of
intercepting the Hart bombers that had

given the Bulldog IIA such a difficult time
and both were fitted with Vickers Mk.V
.303in machine guns.

The last recorded instance of Gauntlets
being used by the RAF was on 1 May 1943
when four of the type were allocated to
1414 Meteorological Flight at Nairobi for
training purposes to alleviate a temporary
shortage of Gladiators.

Gloster Gauntlet production batches:
24 x Gauntlet I del 1.35 to 8.35
(**K4081 - K4104**).*
104 x Gauntlet II del 3.36 to 8.36
(**K5264 - K5367**)
100 x Gauntlet II del 9.36 to 2.37
(**K7792 - K7891**)
*As there was no Gauntlet prototype as
such, K4081 made the type's maiden flight
on 17 December 1934.*

Top left:
As stated with K7793, Gauntlet II K7796 joined 46 Squadron a day prior to the unit's official restoration. Based at Kenley, K7796 appears to be the CO's mount as it has a squadron leader's pennant under the cockpit and a black tip to the fin. The unit's red arrowhead flanked the fuselage roundel while this Gauntlet carries the Fighter Spearhead on its fin. All these aircraft appear to have been fitted with Fairey-Reed three-blade metal propellers. Placed in storage at 24 MU in February 1939, K7796 was shipped to the Middle East in May and stored at Aboukir as a reserve airframe until SOC on 20 April 1940. *Tony O'Toole*

Right:
Not visible in the preceding photographs of 46 Squadron's Gauntlets was the unit's red inward pointing arrowheads set between the roundels on the upper mainplane, both of which can just be recognised in this view of K7843. This view also shows an apparent lack of tonal difference between the forward anodised metal panels and the Aluminium painted fabric areas. K7843 was delivered to the unit on 4 November 1936 remaining until February 1939 when the squadron was poised to re-equip with Hurricanes. Thereafter this Gauntlet was also prepared for service in the Middle East where it went on to serve with 112 Squadron RAF and later 3 Squadron RAAF which certainly used them operationally, albeit briefly, in December 1940. K7843 was SOC on 1 January 1944. While it is known that Gauntlets were used operationally in the Middle East in 1940, they were more usefully employed in the pilot training role to conserve engine hours on the more valuable Gladiator. Having said that, on 7 September 1940, K5355, operated by 430 Flight in East Africa did shoot down a Caproni Ca 133 trimotor.

Right:
K7863 was assigned to 74 Squadron as identified by the unit's narrow black and yellow tiger stripes on the fuselage (obscuring the fuselage serial number), repeated on the upper wing between the roundels. This image also shows what appears to be a black fin, mainwheel discs and tailplanes. A white Fighter Spearhead on the fin contains a tiger head motif taken from the squadron badge as approved by King George VI in February 1937. Scarcely visible on the side of the cockpit is what appears to be a squadron leader's pennant, possibly making this aircraft the personal mount of the unit's CO at the time, Sqn Ldr D S Brookes. K7863 went on to serve with 80 and 74 Squadrons prior to being stored in February 1939; thereafter it was prepared for service in the Middle East where it arrived in June 1939. Held in reserve, K7863 joined 6 Squadron in December and was SOC on 20 April 1940.

Left:
Re-formed in August 1936, these seven 151 Squadron Gauntlets IIs are seen at North Weald in 1937, at a time when their original Watts two-blade wooden propellers were being replaced by Fairey-Reed three-blade metal units. Here, Gauntlets K7890 (nearest the camera), K7832 and K7833 have the new propellers while K5352, K5353 and two others have yet to be converted, a process which also included the need to re-synchronise the guns so as to miss three blades rather than two. The squadron markings feature pale-blue/black/pale-blue bars either side of the fuselage roundels, repeated along the upper wing between the roundels. Presumably the white Fighter Spearhead containing 151's motif – an owl alighting on a seax – has yet to be applied. Of the five identified Gauntlets seen here, K7890 was the last to join 151 Squadron when it arrived in March 1937 and remained until SOC following a forced landing on 2 January 1939; K7833 survived for longer being delivered to the SAAF on 19 July 1940 gaining the serial 873.

Top right:
The camouflaging of RAF aircraft commenced as new aircraft types such as the Hurricane entered service in late 1937, but during the run-up to the Munich Crisis of September 1938, there was a rush to camouflage all RAF combat aircraft already in squadron service resulting in these Gauntlets from 151 Squadron receiving Dark Earth and Dark Green upper surfaces. The introduction of black (officially 'Night') and white under surfaces on new Hurricanes coming off the production line also occurred around this time and Fighter Command were instructed to paint the undersides of the mainplanes of all its fighters in Night and White too, divided down the aircraft centreline. Initially, ailerons were often left in the original Aluminium due to overbalancing concerns. Roundels were also modified by reducing them to just red and blue, ideally using the duller and darker hued, matt, night bomber VNR 5 and VNB 6 paints. In applying the new colour schemes, many aircraft had their serial numbers obscured, hence the identities of these Gauntlets remain unknown.

Centre right:
Gauntlet II K5289 joined 17 Squadron on 3 January 1938 and remained with the unit until sent to 20 MU on 27 June 1939 becoming instructional airframe 3408M in May 1940. In K5289's case it appears that the undersurface of the top wing has been painted in Night, with ailerons on the lower wing painted in opposing Night/White colours. The roundels in all six positions were also toned down by overpainting the White areas in Red and Blue. The serial number appears to have been painted around or re-applied. *Courtesy of Tim Kershaw.*

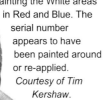

Left:
An unidentified Gauntlet after having obligingly tipped up to reveal its Night and White undersurfaces, its starboard roundel having been over painted in Night. *Tim Kershaw.*

Right:
This unidentified 46 Squadron Gauntlet demonstrates how a given instruction can be misapplied or misunderstood. As can be seen, the Night and White under surfaces should show Night under the port wings and White under the starboard, however, this Gauntlet – seen at Sutton Bridge in the spring of 1939, has them the opposite way around. This Gauntlet carries the pre-war squadron code letters 'RJ' on its fuselage as well as its individual code 'Q' (just visible) in Medium Sea Grey, 46 Squadron having begun to apply their code during October 1938. The underwing roundels appear to have been painted over in black but might in fact be dull shades of red and blue.

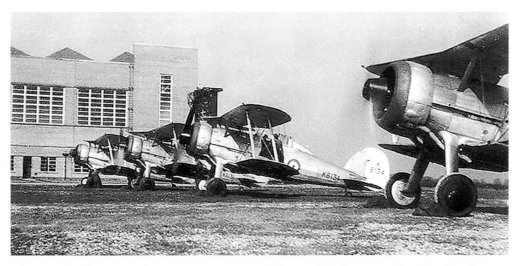

Gloster Gladiator I and II

The Gloster Gladiator became the RAF's last biplane fighter, a type that would introduce certain features which were to become standard on the early monoplane fighters: namely, a fully enclosed cockpit and a significant increase in firepower, which for the Gladiator meant a doubling of the standard gun armament to four fixed machine guns.

The prototype Gladiator, K5200, was initially completed as an open-cockpit machine, although this would alter following subsequent modification, while all production Gladiators had enclosed cockpits. (K5200, first flown on 12 September 1934 was delivered to 1 Squadron for service trials in April 1935 and thereafter spent much of its life on engine, gunnery and gunsight trials until SOC in November 1942.)

The last recorded operational flight of an RAF Gladiator occurred on 7 January 1945 at RAF Ballyhalbert, Northern Ireland, then the home of 1402 Meteorological Flight. Presumably surviving Gladiators made flights after this date if only to return airframes to maintenance units for final disposal.

Gloster Gladiator production batches:
23 x Gladiator I del 2.37 to 4.37
K6129 - K6151

186 x Gladiator I (ordered), 164 del 4.37 to 11.37
K7892 - K8055. K8005 - K8007 went directly to the Iraqi Air Force; K8056 - K8077 cancelled.
16 x Gladiator I del 12.37 to 1.38

L7608 - L7623. Replaced K8005 - K8007 and part replacement for K8056 - K8007).

28 x Gladiator II del 9.38
L8005 - L8032 of which L8005 and L8012 - L8028 were delivered to Royal Egyptian Air Force (REAF) in 4.39

50 x Gladiator II del 12.38 to 2.39
N2265 - N2314. Of these at least 19 were delivered to Worthy Down for transfer to Admiralty charge on 24.5.39, although 28 others did serve with RAF units.

240 x Gladiator II del 3.39 to 4.40
N5575 - N5594; N5620 - N5649; N5680 - N5729; N5750 - N5789; N5810 - N5859; N5875 - N5924.*
At least 46 of the aircraft listed in these

Left:
High above the clouds, K7965 obligingly banks to port to show 73 Squadron's blade-shaped blue bars bordering a yellow centre, flanking the fuselage roundel and positioned in-between the roundels on the upper mainplane to advantage. The squadron only operated Gladiators for just over a year (June 1937 to July 1938) before being equipped with the Hurricane I. Having later served with several home-based fighter squadrons, K7965 was sent to the Middle East in June 1941 where it served with the Communication Flight Air Headquarters Western Desert until SOC on 30 March 1942 following a forced landing a month earlier. The Flight, as might be expected, was tasked with communication duties in the region and as of March 1942 fielded a dozen Lysanders, three Blenheims, three Gladiators, two Hurricanes, two Miles Magisters, a Fieseler Storch and a Bf108.

final production batches were supplied to other nations from RAF stocks, particularly in January 1940, most of which at that time going to the Finish Air Force, the REAF, five to the Norwegians and one to Portugal.
* *Readers might question the absence of Gladiator serial numbers N5500 - N5549 and N5565 - N5574. However, they covered an order for 60 Sea Gladiators delivered directly to the Admiralty and therefore outside the scope of this book.*

Top right:
A pair of 73 Squadron machines as seen through the struts of a Hawker Hart. K7985 was, we believe, being flown by Flying Officer Edgar 'Cobber' Kain, a New Zealander. Kain became an 'ace' during the Battle of France and was officially credited with fourteen victories but was killed on 7 June 1940 when performing a series of low-level aerobatics over Échemines airfield while bidding farewell to his comrades after being ordered back to England for a rest. K7985 later served with 3 Squadron from March 1938, followed by 616, 605 and 263 Squadrons in turn. Stored from late October 1939, it was issued to 2 Anti-Aircraft Cooperation Unit (AACU) on 17 February 1942 with which it served until 28 July 1942 when it collided with Gladiator II L8030 and crashed.

Bottom right:
Eighty-seven Squadron re-formed in March 1937 at Tangmere, initially with Hawker Furies, but on moving to Debden the following June it received Gladiators. K8027 in the foreground is resplendent in a full set of squadron markings including a black fuselage bar (representing a tree) either side of the roundel, with a wavy green line, representing a serpent entwined around it. In WWI, 87 Squadron's identity marking had been a horizontally presented letter 'S' and when it re-formed in March 1937 the 'S' was suitably modified to become a snake. The white fighter spearhead on the fin encloses the unit's stylised snake motif as derived from the unit's original marking. The remainder of the fin appears to be blue indicating the B Flight commander's machine. K8027 was SOC at Benina, Libya, while operating with 1563 Meteorological Flight following a landing accident there on 28 July 1943.

Top right:
Three 87 Squadron Gladiators practice formation flying over Debden while tied together in the summer of 1938. As may be seen, not all RAF biplane fighter squadrons of the period chose to apply unit markings to the upper wings.

Below right:
As UK-based Fighter Squadrons gradually re-equipped with more modern types many surviving Gladiators were despatched to the Middle East to either re-equip existing squadrons or establish new air defence units in the region. K7914 is seen here in the markings of 80 Squadron which re-formed in 1937 at Kenley, initially with Gauntlet IIs, followed by Gladiator Is. In May 1938 the unit arrived at Ismailia, Egypt, to assist with the air defence of the Suez Canal and surrounding areas. Probably photographed at Ismailia in 1939, each Gladiator carried a fighter spearhead on their fin containing a bell – the unit motif – their motto being 'Strike True'. K7914 later went on to operate with 1413 and 1565 Meteorological Flights in Cyprus but came to grief south of Beirut on 25 March 1943, while K7973 (behind) was transferred to the Royal Hellenic Air Force (RHAF) on 15 December 1940.

Gladiator gun progression – From Vickers to Browning

As built, prototype Gladiator K5200, was fitted with two fixed synchronised Vickers .303in machine guns in the forward fuselage with two drum-fed Lewis guns in relatively large fairings located one beneath each lower wing and while the Lewis gun was a fast-firing weapon its magazine only held 97 rounds. That issue was resolved on initial production machines whereby the first few (approximately sixty airframes) were fitted with four fixed Vickers Mk.V .303in machine guns, two in the fuselage with 600 rounds per gun (rpg) and two in flush underwing fairings in lieu of the Lewis guns with 400 rpg. By 1936 the Vickers had become outmoded, their use was a stop-gap solution.

Machine gun conundrum

Prior to the arrival of the Gladiator the RAF had little choice but to equip virtually all its fighters with various Marks of Vickers machine guns. They could be a source of exasperation inasmuch that

vwhile air-cooled versions were adopted for aerial use in WWI, the gun itself was based on the original 500 rounds-per-minute (rpm) infantry weapon – an excellent and formidable design that remained in British Army use into the 1960s. The Air Ministry, aware of the gun's importance in ground fighting, was equally aware that as the speed of aircraft increased in the 1920s, such targets could only remain in a fighter pilot's sights for ever-decreasing periods of time. Thus, steps were taken to increase the gun's ratc of firc to 850 rpm, which ultimately

Left:
An 80 Squadron Gladiator I seen at Ismailia c.1939, still in overall Aluminium finish. The red-coloured fin implies A Flight suggesting this is the flight commander's aircraft. The fighter spearhead complete with bell motif is clearly visible. This particular aircraft was later camouflaged and flown by F/L Marmaduke Thomas St John Pattle, better known as 'Pat' Pattle, the South African-born fighter pilot who is generally considered to be the highest-scoring RAF 'ace' with a total of over 50 'kills'. Later coded 'YK-D', K8011 remained with 80 Squadron until late 1940 by which point the unit had received Gladiator IIs which they retained until March 1941. K8011 was SOC in June 1941.

Right:
A trio of 33 Squadron Gladiator Is photographed in later 1938 at a time when pre-war unit codes were being applied. In 33 Squadron's case the code 'SO' was applied from September 1938, the codes subsequently changing to 'TN' in March 1939 – about the time that the upper surfaces of their Gladiators were camouflaged in Dark Earth and Dark Green – and then to 'NW' upon the outbreak of war in September 1939. The unit claimed its first victories on 14 June 1940 while supporting the British capture of Fort Capuzzo when an Italian Caproni Ca 310 and a Fiat CR.32 were shot down. Of the three Gladiators seen here, the rearmost, K8047, after later serving with 80 Squadron, went to the RHAF in December 1940. L7620 (centre) already has the code 'SO-N' applied to its fuselage in Medium Sea Grey making it difficult to see against the overall Aluminium of the airframe. L7260 went to the RHAF in December 1940, while K8013 (nearest), after serving with 80 Squadron was allocated to the RHAF in May 1941. *Tony O'Toole*

Bottom right:
Displaying one of the fuselage patterns applied 'in service' and mainly to Gladiators during the Munich Crisis, it can just be seen that this anonymous machine also had Night and White under surfaces, although the aileron on the starboard upper mainplane appears to be black. The fuselage roundel has also been modified and toned down by extending the Red and Blue over the White, thus retaining the roundel's original 25 inch diameter. *Tony O'Toole*

Top right:
Gladiator I L7612 from 33 Squadron is seen at Ismailia, Egypt, in 1938 creating its own sandstorm – much to the discomfort of the airman perched on the rear fuselage. Previously a light-bomber squadron, the unit had been the first to fly the Hawker Hart, a fact commemorated by the unit's hart motif seen in the fighter spearhead on L7612's fin. On 1 March 1938, 33 Squadron was reorganized as a fighter unit to become the only single-seat fighter squadron outside the UK at that time. Eventually, as home-based fighter units re-equipped with monoplanes, it became possible to despatch quantities of Gladiators (and some Gauntlets) to reinforce the Middle East, East Africa and Aden and thus provide a core of fighter cover. Later allocated to K Flight* operating from Summit, Sudan, L7612 was badly damaged in combat with Italian Fiat CR.42 biplane fighters in November 1940, the subsequent crash-landing writing the Gladiator off.
* Historically K Flight has had at least three iterations, the first was in July 1918 when it operated as a detached flight from 6 Squadron flying RE.8s on the Western Front. The second confirmed occasion was on 1 September 1940 when B Flight of 112 Squadron was detached to the Sudan and redesignated as K Flight. The Flight was disbanded on 1 April 1941 in Palestine when 250 Squadron re-formed. (For the record, K Flight re-formed at Melton Mowbray as freight unit equipped with the Short Stirling V in September 1945.)

Centre right:
Gladiator I, L7614, also from 33 Squadron is refuelled in Egypt in 1938. The flush-fitting underwing gun fairing is shown to advantage in this view, although the gun itself is not installed. L7614 was shot down by CR.42s on 6 November 1940 near the Ethiopian town of Metemma on the Ethiopian/Sudanese border. *Tony O'Toole*

resulted in the Vickers Mk.III. Regrettably, this had the effect of decreasing the reliability of both the gun and its associated components, with frequent stoppages caused by mis-feeds as the ammunition feed proved to be slower than the gun's firing mechanism which in turn placed additional stresses on other components often causing them to fail too. Whatever the deficiencies of the Mk.III overall, its situation wasn't helped by the need to use vast stocks of ageing ammunition in which the propellant (cordite), deteriorating with age, could render a cartridge non-functional or even dangerous. Which is why breech blocks had to be placed close by a fighter pilot, some of whom carried a mallet in the hope that a hefty blow might clear a stoppage.

There were other reasons why it was becoming necessary to increase rates of fire, particularly in fighters. A steady change from wood to metal construction in combination with increasingly powerful powerplants presented the likelihood of armour being added to future military aircraft, thus furthering doubts as to whether a single pair of rifle-calibre guns would still be effective. Because trials with .5in rounds during the 1920s proved disappointing it was eventually determined that the RAF should continue using rifle-calibre weapons, albeit faster-firing ones, with future fighters mounting multiple .303in weapons which today usually conjures up images of the eight-gun monoplane: sadly history tends to forget the Gladiator which was the RAF's first multi-gun fighter, i.e. one equipped with more than just two fixed forward firing guns as standard.

Enter the Browning machine gun. To cut a complex story short, following a decade of indecision concerning.5in versus .303in, six Brownings were acquired and extensively tested until, in 1934, approval was given for sufficient '1930 Pattern' .303 Brownings to be obtained to equip two squadrons for extended trials. As we now know the choice of gun proved to be correct; it was very reliable and with a cyclic rate of 1,100 rpm a fast firing one. Not wishing to be excluded from participating in the trials and tests, Vickers developed their Mk.IIIS machine gun which later became the Vickers Mk.V. Despite or because its cyclic rate was reduced to approximately 720 rpm, the Mk.V featured breech tolerances able to tolerate the ageing sub-standard .303in ammunition manufactured twenty years earlier resulting in what became a much more reliable weapon, albeit one that still could not match the Browning's reliability nor rate of fire. Having made mention of the ammunition, it does beg the question: did the introduction of new Brownings lead to the manufacture of new ammunition, or were they expected to make do with the ageing rounds already discussed? A question this author has not been able to answer.

Whilst the Browning supplanted the Vickers, the equally venerable Lewis gun was supplanted by the drum-fed Vickers Gas Operated (VGO) .303in machine gun which by the start of WWII was a standard fit on most multi-seat *monoplane* bombers as well as being mounted in the Blenheim If's turret. The 'VGO' had a cyclic rate of 1,050 rpm and weighed 19lbs.

Top left:
A worm's-eye view of camouflaged Gladiator I, K7958 'OP-Q', showing Night/White under surfaces with centreline demarcation, although the underside of the ailerons appear to have been left in Aluminium. The pre-war code 'OP' identifies K7958 as a 3 Squadron machine that was photographed at Sutton Bridge on 6 February 1939. Originally 3 Squadron operated Gladiators until March 1938 when Hurricanes replaced them, however, due to a fatal crash at Kenley, their home station, Kenley was deemed too small to operate Hurricanes and so they reverted to Gladiators in July 1938. Following a move to Biggin Hill, the unit again received Hurricanes from May 1939. Note that the Gladiator's black under surfaces are the reverse of those applied to Gauntlet 'RJ-Q'. K7958 was passed to 615 Squadron on 19 June 1939 but came to an untimely end two weeks later when, following an engine failure it struck trees on 2 July and was written off.

Below:
Following the declaration of war in 1939, the RAF sent two Gladiator units, 607 and 615 Squadrons, to France as part of the Air Component of the British Expeditionary Force (BEF). In this image detached 615 Squadron Gladiator IIs are seen at St. Inglevert, France, in late 1939, their codes having changed from 'RR' to 'KW' upon declaration of war. Judging by the upper surface camouflage pattern these are older machines painted 'in-house' simply by applying Dark Earth and Dark Green in a variation of the Air Diagram Camouflage Scheme developed for twin engine monoplanes, rather than the four-colour Shadow Compensating Scheme specifically introduced for biplanes. As may be seen, Red/Blue upper wing roundels were retained but, as an aid to recognition, the fuselage roundels were modified to Red/White/Blue – a post November 1939 modification. The small light-coloured square on the starboard lower mainplane is a gas warning patch. The unit's conversion to Hurricanes began one flight at a time in April 1940, although twelve or more Gladiators are believed to have remained on strength when the German offensive was launched on 10 May.

Gloster Gauntlet I, K4092, 19 Sqn, RAF Duxford, early 1935
No.19 Squadron started re-equipment with Gauntlet Is in January 1935, having previously flown Bulldog IIAs. K4092 joined the squadron on 4th March 1935 and served until 8th November 1935 when it was damaged beyond repair. 19 Squadron's blue and white checks straddled the fuselage roundels and between the roundels on the upper wing which were of 35in diameter and no longer overlapped the ailerons. The squadron's 'Wing'd Dolphin' badge was displayed on the fin within a blue shield rather than the official Fighter spearhead. The red mainwheel hubs may be a Flight marking.

Gloster Gauntlet II, K5359, 17 Sqn, RAF Kenley, May 1937
The Gauntlet II was externally identical to the Mk.I but constructed using bolted and riveted steel tube and duralumin framework which was easier to build and repair than the Mk.I's original welded structure. Delivered to 17 Squadron in August 1936, K5359 features the unit's parallel zig-zag bars on the fuselage which were repeated on the upper wing between the roundels – again of 35in diameter and not overlapping the ailerons (see plan view opposite). 17 Squadron's Gauntlets invariably featured black fuselage top decking, but K5359 had red decking which was probably a Flight colour (like the mainwheel hubs) indicating a Flight Commander. The squadron's gauntlet was carried on the fin within a white Fighter Spearhead. K5359 crashed at Kenley on 8th May 1939.

Gloster Gauntlet II, K7824, 66 Sqn, RAF Duxford, mid 1937
Re-formed, (from C Flight, 19 Squadron), on 20th July 1936, 66 Squadron operated Gauntlet IIs until re-equipped with Spitfire Is over the winter of 1938/39. K7824 carries the unit's markings of two tapering pale blue bars   outlined with a thin black border on the fuselage sides from the cockpit to the tailplane, straddling the roundel. Two similar pale blue bars thinly outlined in black, but parallel not tapered, were carried on the upper wing, between the roundels – (see plan view opposite) – but it is uncertain if all 66 Squadron Gauntlets had them applied. Again the mainwheel hubs are red indicating a Flight marking. The squadron's coiled rattlesnake within a white Fighter spearhead was applied to the fin. K7824 went on to serve with 615 Squadron before becoming an Instructional Airframe 2250M in May 1940.

Representative wing upper surface Squadron markings

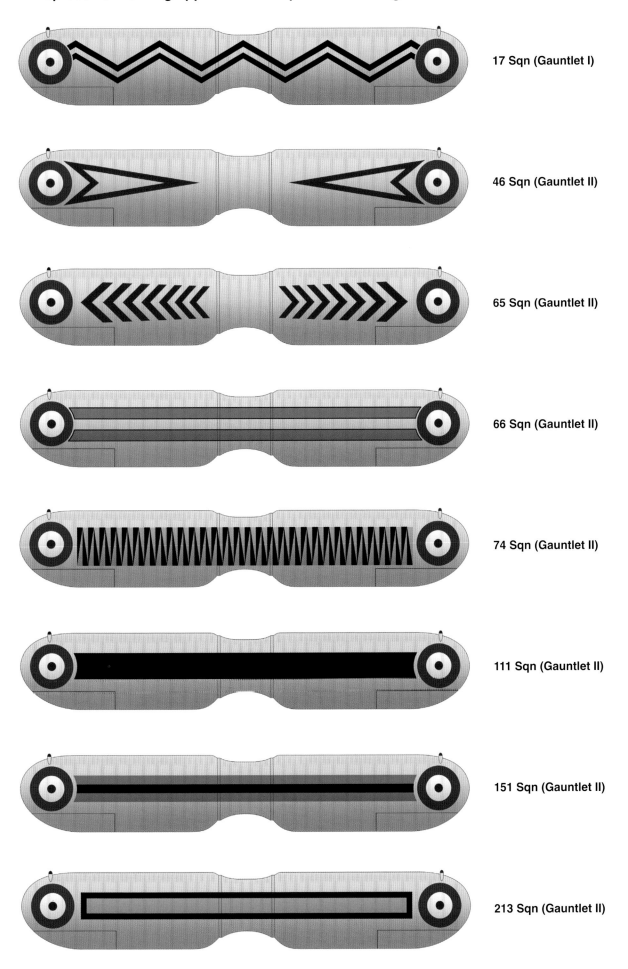

17 Sqn (Gauntlet I)

46 Sqn (Gauntlet II)

65 Sqn (Gauntlet II)

66 Sqn (Gauntlet II)

74 Sqn (Gauntlet II)

111 Sqn (Gauntlet II)

151 Sqn (Gauntlet II)

213 Sqn (Gauntlet II)

Gloster Gauntlet II, K7863, 74 Sqn, RAF Hornchurch, circa 1937/38
One of the most distinctive squadron marking designs was carried by 74's Gauntlets, illustrated here on K7863. The black and yellow vertical triangles, resembling Tiger stripes, were applied along the fuselage sides from cockpit to tailplane (obscuring the fuselage serial number) and repeated on the upper wing between the roundels (see plan view on previous page). Believed to have been the personal mount of the unit's CO at the time, S/Ldr D S Brookes, a Squadron Leader's pennant was applied under the cockpit coaming and the aircraft had a black fin and tailplanes edged in yellow, and black mainwheel discs similarly outlined in yellow. The white Fighter spearhead on the fin featured the Tiger's head from the squadron badge as approved by King George VI in February 1937.

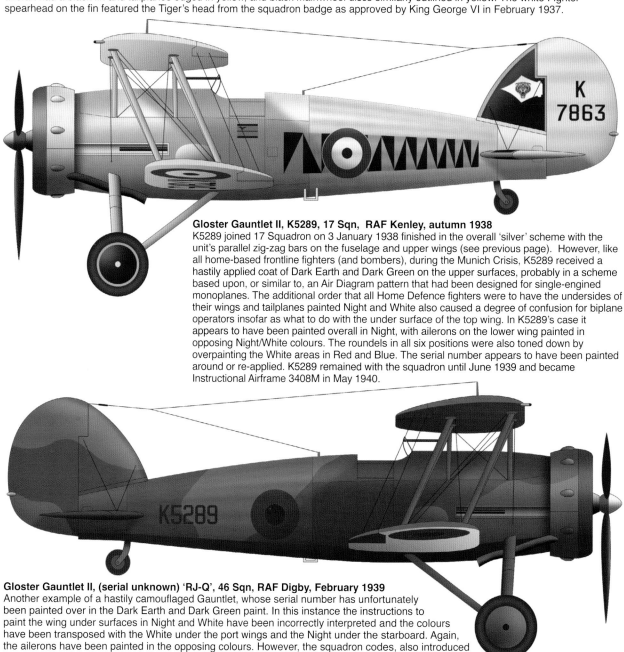

Gloster Gauntlet II, K5289, 17 Sqn, RAF Kenley, autumn 1938
K5289 joined 17 Squadron on 3 January 1938 finished in the overall 'silver' scheme with the unit's parallel zig-zag bars on the fuselage and upper wings (see previous page). However, like all home-based frontline fighters (and bombers), during the Munich Crisis, K5289 received a hastily applied coat of Dark Earth and Dark Green on the upper surfaces, probably in a scheme based upon, or similar to, an Air Diagram pattern that had been designed for single-engined monoplanes. The additional order that all Home Defence fighters were to have the undersides of their wings and tailplanes painted Night and White also caused a degree of confusion for biplane operators insofar as what to do with the under surface of the top wing. In K5289's case it appears to have been painted overall in Night, with ailerons on the lower wing painted in opposing Night/White colours. The roundels in all six positions were also toned down by overpainting the White areas in Red and Blue. The serial number appears to have been painted around or re-applied. K5289 remained with the squadron until June 1939 and became Instructional Airframe 3408M in May 1940.

Gloster Gauntlet II, (serial unknown) 'RJ-Q', 46 Sqn, RAF Digby, February 1939
Another example of a hastily camouflaged Gauntlet, whose serial number has unfortunately been painted over in the Dark Earth and Dark Green paint. In this instance the instructions to paint the wing under surfaces in Night and White have been incorrectly interpreted and the colours have been transposed with the White under the port wings and the Night under the starboard. Again, the ailerons have been painted in the opposing colours. However, the squadron codes, also introduced during the Munich Crisis, had been applied correctly, 46 Squadron's pre-war code 'RJ' applied on one side of the fuselage roundel and the individual aircraft letter 'Q' on the other side, both in Medium Sea Grey.

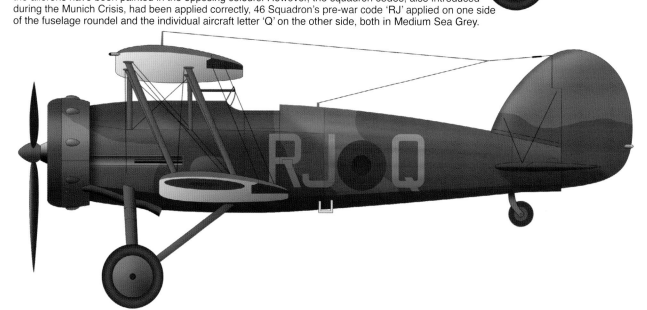

Gloster Gladiator I, K6145, 3 Sqn, RAF Kenley, March 1937
No. 3 Squadron became the second unit to equip with Gladiators in March 1937 having previously
been equipped with Bulldog IIAs. Finished in the overall 'silver' scheme, the unit continued to apply
their distinctive emerald green bar flanking the fuselage roundel, but this time in truncated tapering
form with a rounded front. Similarly the emerald green bar repeated on the upper wing was tapered
towards the roundels. The mainwheel hubs are red, probably denoting A Flight. K6145, thought to
have been armed with Vickers Mk.V machine guns under the wing, served with several units, the last
being 263 Squadron from 10 October 1939, until eleven days later when it hit the surface of the River
Severn in Gloucestershire and blew up.

Gloster Gladiator I, K7985, 73 Sqn, RAF Debden, spring 1938
Having briefly operated Fury IIs, 73 re-equipped with Gladiators in June 1937 and
applied its distinctive yellow and blue tapered flash marking to the fuselage, repeating
the design on the upper wing surfaces (see plan views overleaf). K7985 is thought to
have been flown by F/O Edgar 'Cobber' Kain, (a New Zealander who became an 'ace'
during the Battle of France with fourteen victories, but was tragically killed on 7 June
1940 in a flying accident. K7985 later served with 3, 616, 605 and 263 Squadrons in
turn. Stored from late October 1939, it was issued to 2 Anti-Aircraft Cooperation Unit
(AACU) on 17 February 1942 with which it served until 28 July 1942 when it collided
with Gladiator II L8030 and crashed.

Gloster Gladiator I, K8027, 87 Sqn, RAF Debden, 1937/38
Reformed in March 1937 at Tangmere, where it was briefly equipped with Hawker
Furies, on moving to Debden in the June, 87 Squadron received Gladiator Is. K8027
carries its squadron markings on the fuselage sides, flanking the roundel, comprising a
horizontal black bar with a wavy green line, (representing a snake from the Squadron's
badge). No markings were carried on the top wing upper surfaces. The fin is blue,
indicating the B Flight commander's machine, with a white Fighter spearhead enclosing
the unit's stylised snake motif. K8027 was SOC at Benina, Libya, while operating with
1563 Meteorological Flight following a landing accident there on 28 July 1943.

Gladiator I, K8011, 80 Sqn, RAF Amriya, Egypt, early 1939
Reformed at Kenley in March 1937, with a mix of Gauntlets and Gladiators, 80 Squadron soon mainstreamed on Gladiator Is moving to Henlow and then Debden before going overseas, to Egypt, in May 1938, to join 33 Squadron to form a Gladiator Wing tasked with defending the Suez Canal. Based at Amriya in early 1939, K8011 was still in overall Aluminium 'silver' finish, and devoid of any squadron markings, but featured a red-coloured fin implying 'A Flight' and possibly the Flight Commander's aircraft, and red mainwheel hubs. The white Fighter spearhead contained the squadron's bell. K8011 was later camouflaged and flown by F/L Marmaduke Thomas St John 'Pat' Pattle, the South African-born fighter pilot who is generally considered to be the highest-scoring RAF 'ace' with a total of over 50 'kills'. Later coded 'YK-D', K8011 is thought to have remained with 80 Squadron until late 1940. K8011 was SOC in June 1941.

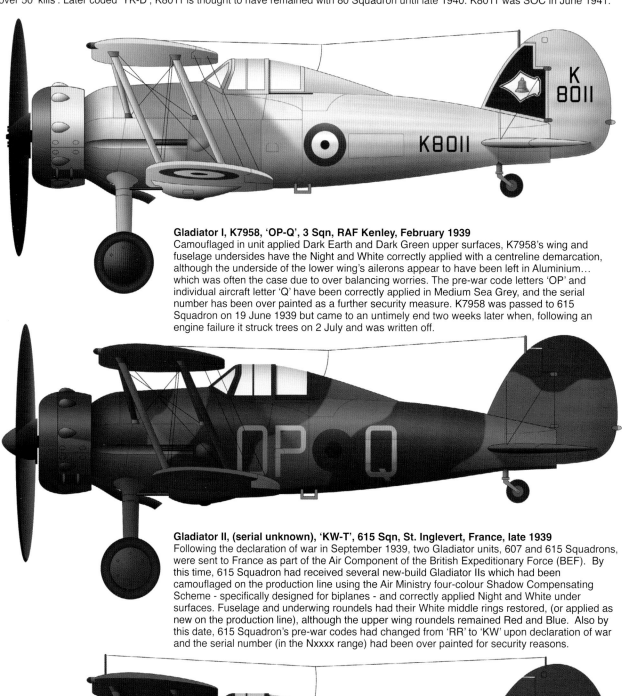

Gladiator I, K7958, 'OP-Q', 3 Sqn, RAF Kenley, February 1939
Camouflaged in unit applied Dark Earth and Dark Green upper surfaces, K7958's wing and fuselage undersides have the Night and White correctly applied with a centreline demarcation, although the underside of the lower wing's ailerons appear to have been left in Aluminium… which was often the case due to over balancing worries. The pre-war code letters 'OP' and individual aircraft letter 'Q' have been correctly applied in Medium Sea Grey, and the serial number has been over painted as a further security measure. K7958 was passed to 615 Squadron on 19 June 1939 but came to an untimely end two weeks later when, following an engine failure it struck trees on 2 July and was written off.

Gladiator II, (serial unknown), 'KW-T', 615 Sqn, St. Inglevert, France, late 1939
Following the declaration of war in September 1939, two Gladiator units, 607 and 615 Squadrons, were sent to France as part of the Air Component of the British Expeditionary Force (BEF). By this time, 615 Squadron had received several new-build Gladiator IIs which had been camouflaged on the production line using the Air Ministry four-colour Shadow Compensating Scheme - specifically designed for biplanes - and correctly applied Night and White under surfaces. Fuselage and underwing roundels had their White middle rings restored, (or applied as new on the production line), although the upper wing roundels remained Red and Blue. Also by this date, 615 Squadron's pre-war codes had changed from 'RR' to 'KW' upon declaration of war and the serial number (in the Nxxxx range) had been over painted for security reasons.

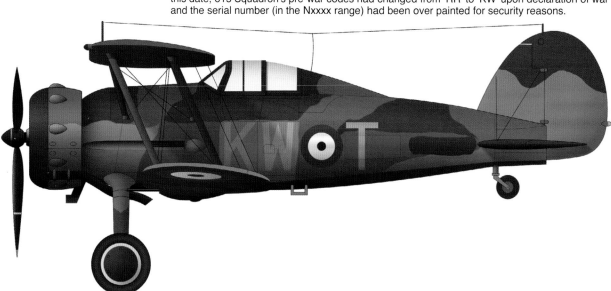

Representative wing upper surface Squadron markings

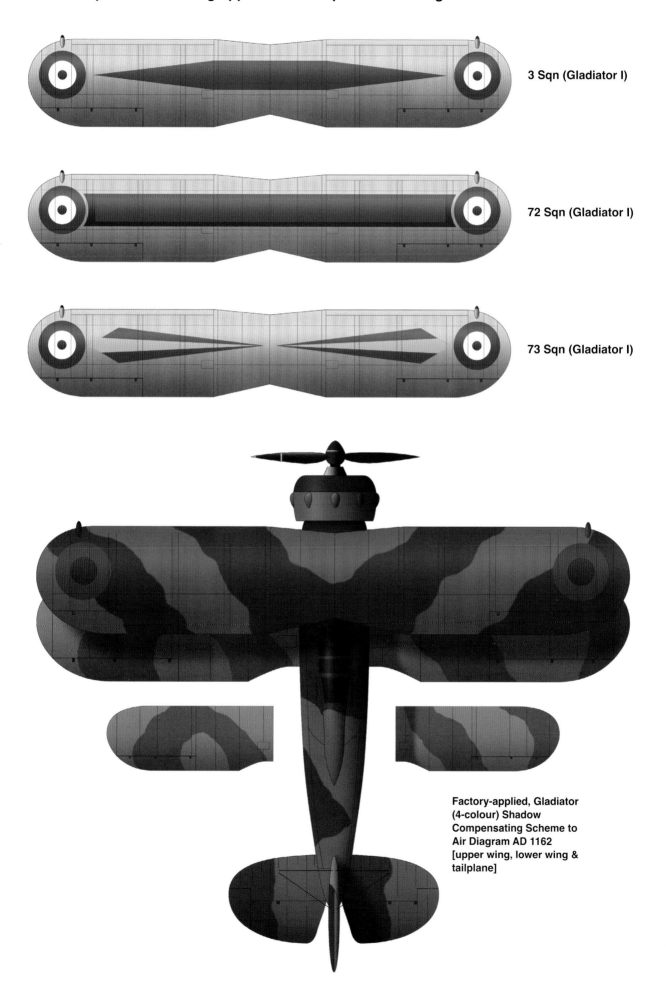

3 Sqn (Gladiator I)

72 Sqn (Gladiator I)

73 Sqn (Gladiator I)

Factory-applied, Gladiator
(4-colour) Shadow
Compensating Scheme to
Air Diagram AD 1162
[upper wing, lower wing &
tailplane]

Hurricane I, L1559, 111 Sqn, RAF Northolt, mid-1938
The first frontline squadron to re-equip with the Hurricane was 111 Squadron, which had relinquished its Gauntlets by February 1938. Hurricanes were finished in the then newly adopted Temperate Land Scheme of Dark Earth and Dark Green upper surfaces, to one of two patterns, A Scheme or B Scheme (mirror images of each other applied to alternating airframes on the production line), with Aluminium under surfaces. L1559 was finished in the A Scheme. Initially, fuselage serial numbers were incorrectly applied in 6 inch high characters instead of the official 8 inches, an anomaly that was rectified on later airframes. 30 inch high serial numbers were carried under the wings reading from the front under the port wing and from the rear under the starboard wing. The squadron badge was carried on both sides of the fin, usually within a standard frame, but in L1559's case, it was surrounded by a red 'Fighter' spearhead. During this pre-Munich Crisis period, 111's squadron number was applied in white numerals, with the top half in the Flight colour… in L1559's case, red for A Flight.

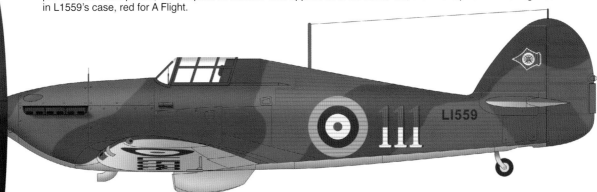

Hurricane I, L1634, 'NO-L' 85 Sqn, RAF Debden, winter 1938/39
L1634 was finished in the B Scheme upper surface camouflage pattern, with correctly painted Night/White under surfaces divided down the centreline. Its upper wing and fuselage roundels had the Yellow outer rings over painted in camouflage colours and the White inner ring over painted by extending the areas of Red and Blue, to create Red/Blue roundels, the freshly-applied paint often being noticeable. As an added security measure on many aircraft the fuselage serial number was also over painted, as in L1634's case. Code letters, which were introduced in the summer of 1938, were applied at squadron level, in Medium Sea Grey. Although they were officially to be 48 inches high, even the Hurricane which had deeper fuselage sides than the previous generation of biplanes, and indeed the forthcoming Spitfire, could only accommodate code letters of a maximum of 36 to 40 inches high, and many Hurricane squadrons applied smaller code letters, such as these seen on L1634. By this period Hurricanes were being fitted with ejector exhaust manifolds which replaced the so called 'kidney' exhausts. L1634 struck a ditch and overturned on 20 December 1938 after its engine cut while departing Debden and became instructional airframe 1358M as a consequence.

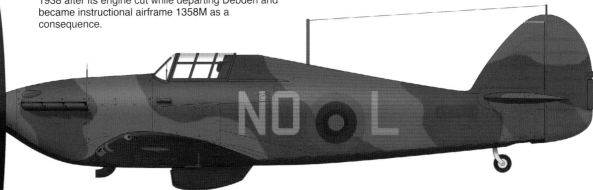

Hurricane I, L1719, 'AL-F', 79 Sqn, RAF Biggin Hill, spring 1939
79 Squadron applied slightly bigger code letters to its Hurricanes as illustrated by L1719 which retained its serial number on the rear fuselage, albeit in 6 inch high digits. Finished in the A Scheme camouflage pattern, this aircraft also featured toned-down Red/Blue roundels on the wing upper surfaces and fuselage sides. Again the Night/White under surfaces are correctly divided down the centreline with no under wing roundels applied. An exception to the no roundels under the Night/White wings rule was covered in AMO A.520, dated 7 December 1939, which stated that Fighter aircraft stationed in France were to carry Red/White/Blue roundels under the wings. L1719 only served with 79 Squadron and was Damaged Beyond Repair (DBR) at Biggin Hill in April 1940 following a forced landing.

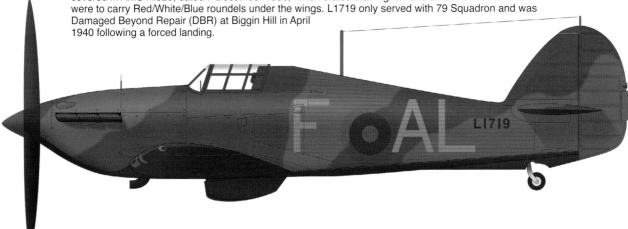

Hurricane Air Diagram AD 1160 upper surface plan views

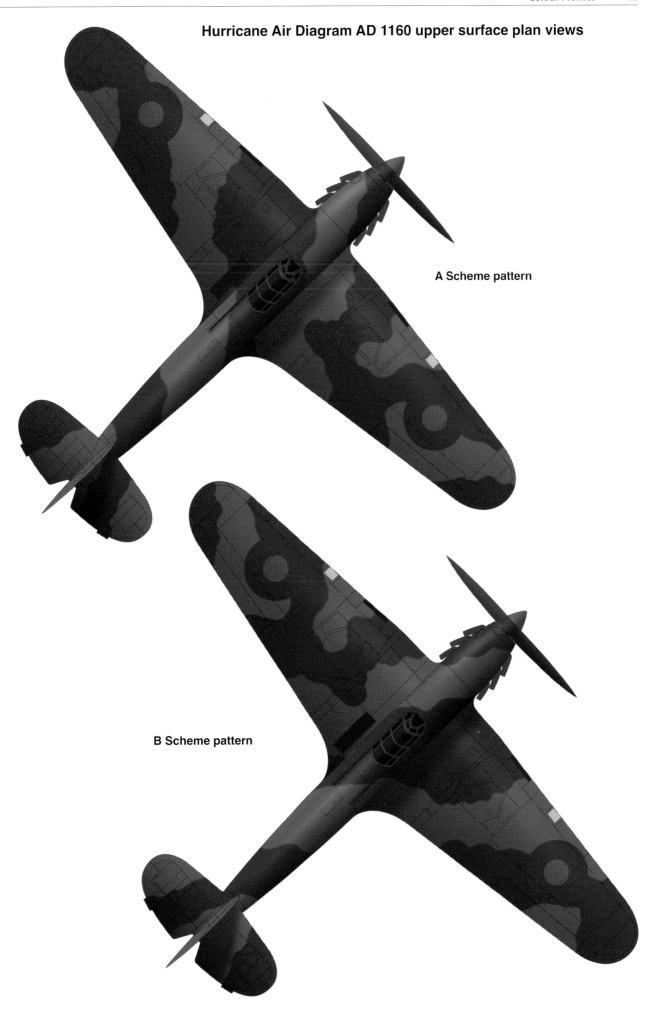

A Scheme pattern

B Scheme pattern

Spitfire I, K9797, '19' from 19 Sqn, RAF Duxford, October 1938
The first squadron to receive Spitfires was 19, in August 1938, just before the Munich Crisis. On 8 October, six of the unit's aircraft attended a display for the opening of Cambridge Airport, for which the numeral '19' was applied to their fins. K9797, the CO's (S/Ldr Henry Cozens) aircraft, had a red '19' applied, with other five having white '19's – the fin markings only lasted a few days before being removed. K9797, was finished in Dark Earth and Dark Green upper surfaces to the A Scheme pattern with Aluminium under surfaces, and was still wearing pre-Munich high-visibility roundels. Fitted with a spin recovery parachute guard at the top of the fin, K9797 only served with 19 Squadron and was DBR after a forced landing at Acton in Suffolk on 9 September 1939.

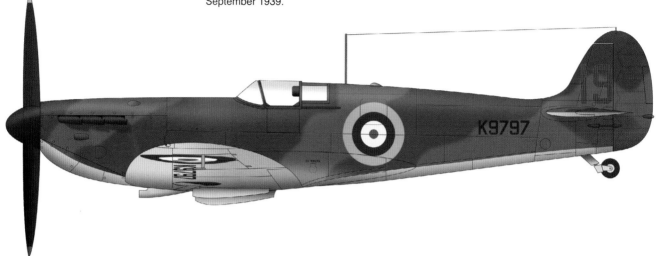

Spitfire I, K9906, 'FZ-L', 65 Sqn, RAF Hornchurch, mid-1939
Like 'SD-H', K9906 carries the squadron's pre-war code 'FZ' which changed to 'YT' from September 1939. Finished in the A Scheme upper surfaces, K9906 had its Night/White under surfaces applied 'in service' but were again correctly divided down the fuselage centreline. Although overpainted, the fuselage serial number K9906 is just discernible but was repeated in miniature on the fin. Freshly applied areas of Dark Earth and Dark Green are apparent around the fuselage roundel, modified to 25 inches in diameter in Red/Blue in lieu of the previous Red/White/Blue/Yellow style. K9906 was purportedly flown by the then F/O Robert Stanford Tuck (who would later achieve twenty-seven aerial victories plus two shared). The aircraft has a de Havilland metal propeller and spinner and a domed canopy hood with the oval punch-out panel. K9906 later became 'YT-T' and later served with 64 Squadron and 7 OTU, before being converted to PR.I standard and service with 1 PRU.

Spitfire I, (serial overpainted), 'SD-H', 72 Sqn, RAF Church Fenton, April 1939
With the introduction of code letters and low visibility Red/Blue roundels due to the Munich Crisis, like all RAF aircraft, Spitfires soon took on a more sombre look. 72 Squadron started receiving Spitfires in April 1939, at around the same time that Supermarine were delivering them off the production line with correctly applied Night/White under surfaces, divided down the fuselage centreline as illustrated here. There was a slight difference between in-service modified roundels which were modified by using the outer edge of the Blue ring as the outer diameter, (the Yellow ring being completely over painted in the surrounding camouflage colours), and extending the Red and Blue over the White, resulting in the fuselage roundels being 25 inches diameter and the upper wing roundels 40 inches in diameter, as in this illustration, and production applied roundels that were 15 inches diameter on the fuselage and 35 inches diameter above the wings. 'SD-H', finished in the B Scheme, still carried the squadron's badge, a Swift (symbolic of speed), within a 'Fighter' spearhead on the fin.

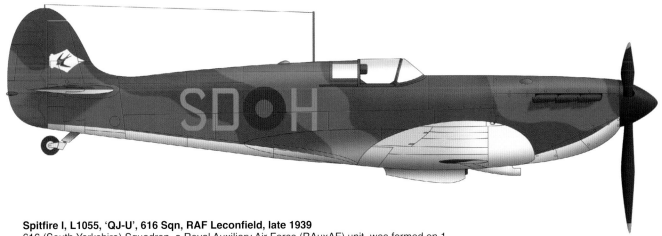

Spitfire I, L1055, 'QJ-U', 616 Sqn, RAF Leconfield, late 1939
616 (South Yorkshire) Squadron, a Royal Auxiliary Air Force (RAuxAF) unit, was formed on 1 November 1938 initially in the bomber role, which changed when Gloster Gauntlets were received in January 1939. Fairey Battle light bombers were delivered in May 1939 for Merlin engine experience to assist the squadron in preparing for re-equipment with Spitfire Is in October 1939, when the squadron moved to RAF Leconfield and by the end of November conversion to the modern fighter was complete. Originally allocated to 66 Squadron, by late 1939, L1055 had been transferred to 616 Squadron, which was still using its pre-war codes 'QJ'.

Due to a tragic recognition mistake which resulted in the accidental shooting down of an Avro Anson coastal reconnaissance aircraft by a section of 602 Squadron Spitfires on 24 October 1939, following Air Ministry trials, from late November/early December 1939, all RAF aircraft were to have Red/White/Blue roundels on the fuselage sides, resulting in L1055 having its 25 inch diameter Red/Blue roundels modified back to Red/White/Blue by the addition of a white centre ring. Finished in the Temperate Land Scheme of Dark Earth and Dark Green upper surfaces, to the B Scheme, L1055 featured 'in service' repainted under surfaces comprising Night/White mainplane and tailplane under surfaces with Aluminium nose and rear fuselage.

Also, like most Spitfires of this period, the upper/under surface demarcation on the nose followed the curve of the cowling under surface contours rather than the straight panel line as on later Spitfires. L1055 was fitted with a de Havilland metal propeller and spinner and had a domed canopy hood fitted with the oval punch-out panel which was designed to equalise air pressure inside the cockpit in an emergency.

Note: The pre-war codes 'QJ' were retained by 616 Squadron until October 1941 by which point the squadron had been flying the Spitfire IIa for several months, when they were correctly coded 'YQ'. Confusingly, although 92 Squadron had been allocated the codes 'QJ' upon the outbreak of war, it also retained its pre-war 'GR' codes until May/June 1940.

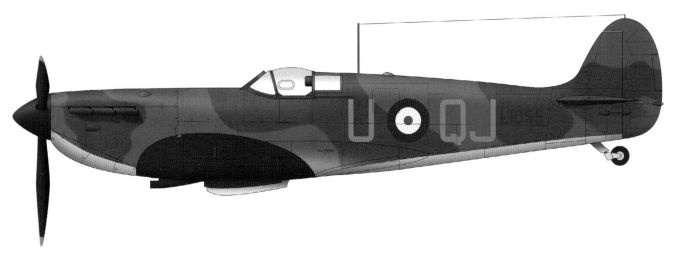

Miles M.24 Master Fighter, N7412, Woodley Aerodrome, Berkshire, 1940
What might have been… the Miles M.24 Master Fighter. This was a proposal for an emergency design created in early 1940, by the designers at Phillips & Powis Aircraft Ltd, (who produced Miles aircraft), as a stop-gap fighter. Modified from the existing Miles M.9 Master I Trainer, which entered service in 1939, and powered by a 715hp Rolls Royce Kestrel XXX inline engine, with the rear seat removed and three .303 inch Browning machine-guns mounted in each wing. N7412 is believed to be the prototype that was modified for, but probably not with, the six guns.

N7412 was finished in the standard Dark Earth/Dark Green Temperate Land Scheme upper surfaces, to Air Diagram AD 1160 for Single Engine Monoplanes, in the A Scheme, with Yellow undersides to Pattern No. 2, (i.e. high up on the fuselage sides). The rudder was also Yellow. The propeller spinner was polished natural metal. N7412 may have been the only one of the 23 airframes that were earmarked for conversion, (N7412 and N7801 to N7822), to have actually had the 'fighter' modifications implemented. Some references quote that after the rear seat and some of the equipment had been removed from N7412, preliminary test flights showed that the aircraft was slow (with a maximum speed of 226 mph) but manoeuvrable and easy to control. Neither N7412 (nor any of the other earmarked airframes) ever saw combat. N7412 was ultimately allocated to various Flying Training Schools (FTSs) before diving in to ground near RAF Babtown Farm, Gloucestershire, on 23 July 1941. All the other earmarked airframes (N7801 to N7822) were used in training, serving with various Operational Training Units (OTUs) and FTSs.

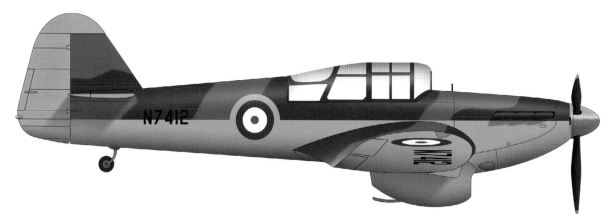

Blenheim If, L8372, 'YB-L', 29 Sqn, RAF Debden, early 1939
No Blenheims were built as Fighters on the production line, but as the type proved to be faster than the RAF's biplane fighters (i.e. Gauntlets and Gladiators), and required little in the way of modification, approximately 200 Blenheim I bombers were converted to become Mk.If fighters by the simple expedient of fitting a ventral gun tray containing four .303 Browning machine guns under the bomb bay. The first squadron to receive the new 'fighter' was 25, in October 1938, with 29 Squadron following in the December. Like all Blenheim Is, L8372 was finished in the standard AD 1159 Twin Engine Monoplane (Medium Bombers), Dark Earth/Dark Green Temperate Land Scheme, in this case to the A Scheme pattern, with Night under surfaces on the production line. The roundels have been toned-down to the Red/Blue style and the serial number painted out on the fuselage and rudder, and under the wings, although it is thought that, at the time of this illustration, the White starboard under wing had yet to be applied. L8372 went on to serve with 604 and 600 Squadrons before becoming Instructional Airframe, 3195M, in April 1941.

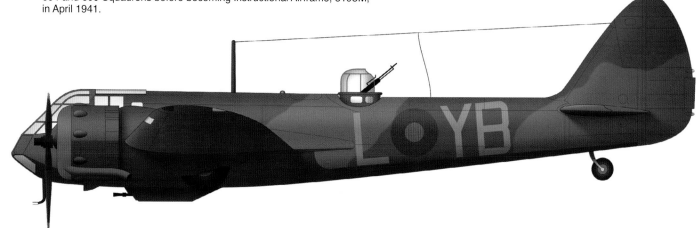

Blenheim If, (serial overpainted), 'YN-B', 601 Sqn, RAF Hendon, early 1939
601 Squadron exchanged its Gauntlet IIs for Blenheim Ifs in January 1939. Finished in the standard
AD 1159 Dark Earth/Dark Green Temperate Land Scheme, again to the A Scheme pattern, with
Night under surfaces, in this instance it is thought that the White starboard under wing HAD been
applied, although the engine cowling underside may have remained in Night, a common anomaly
seen on many Blenheim I 'fighters'. (see 'UF-D' below). With toned-down Red/Blue roundels and
painted out serial number on the fuselage, rudder and under the wings, the squadron's winged
sword was still carried on the fin within a fighter spearhead, albeit just in red, and the aircraft's
individual code letter 'B' was repeated on the cockpit nose panel.

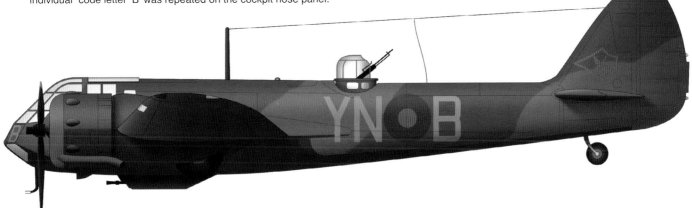

Blenheim If, (serial overpainted), 'UF-D', 601 Sqn, RAF Biggin Hill, late 1939
Upon the outbreak of war in September 1939, 601 Squadron's pre-war code 'YN' was changed to 'UF'. 'UF-D' was
finished in the B Scheme upper surface camouflage pattern with modified 47½ inch Red/Blue upper wing roundels
and fuselage roundels modified to the Red/White/Blue style of 35 inch diameter. The code letters are
approximately 40 inches high in Medium Sea Grey. Night/White under surfaces had become well established by
this time, however, as with the single-engined fighters, Blenheim fighters displayed several variations including just
having the starboard wing under surface painted White, or as in the case of 'UF-D', correctly divided down the
fuselage centreline, although again, the starboard engine cowling underside remained in Night as did the starboard
aileron and the tailplane and elevator to record another variation on the Night/White Scheme. 601 Squadron was
equipped with Blenheim fighters until February 1940 when they were replaced by the Hurricane I.

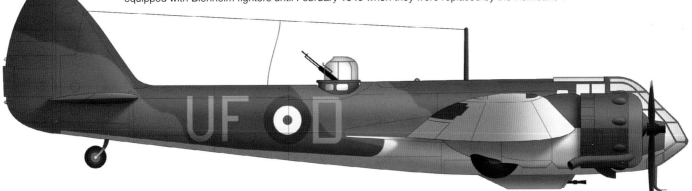

Blenheim If, K7048, 'ZK-U', 25 Sqn, RAF North Weald, late 1939
By the end of 1939, twenty squadrons had, or were in the process of, re-equipping with the Blenheim fighter, and
by this time most had their pre-war codes changed, with 25 Squadron replacing 'RX' with 'ZK'. K7048 was also
finished in the B Scheme upper surface camouflage pattern with 47½ inch Red/Blue upper wing roundels and 35
inch Red/White/Blue fuselage roundels. Code letters were in Medium Sea Grey and approximately 48 inches high.
In this instance, the starboard engine cowling underside was painted White, but interestingly, the upper/under
surface demarcation under the wing root was at a sharp angle rather than the standard radius curve. K7048 had
previously served as a bomber with 90 and 101 Squadrons, before modification to fighter standard, and went on to
serve with 236 Squadron before returning to 25, and seeing its days out with the Beam Approach Training Flight
and then 17 OTU with whom it was serving when dived into the ground on approach to RAF Upwood in October
1941. All Blenheim Ifs retained the single fixed Browning located in the port wing plus a single .303 Vickers 'K'
machine gun in a dorsal turret, both being standard on Blenheim bombers at this time.

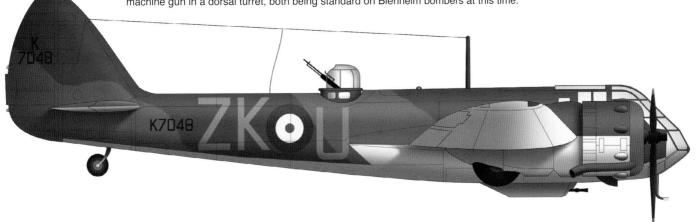

The monoplane fighters: 1936-1939

Above:
The solitary Hurricane prototype, K5083, as seen prior to its first flight on 6 November 1935. By comparison with production Hurricanes the points of interest include the single canopy stiffener, tailplane struts, and the short-lived D-shaped wheel covers which hinged at 90 degrees to the undercarriage legs but suffered damage when taxying over rough grass. Originally intended to be fitted with four Vickers .303in machine guns (two in the nose and two in the wings), the specification was later modified to accept eight Brownings, although when this photo was taken no weapons were fitted.
Tony Buttler collection

Few readers will require an introduction to either the Hurricane or the Spitfire, nonetheless it is worth pondering just how few of either type existed pre-war. By the end of 1938 eleven Hurricane squadrons had formed, but for the Spitfire the situation was worse and while it is true that two squadrons did receive this complex fighter in 1938 their numbers remained low with just fourteen squadrons being equipped with the type by late December 1939; at which time the number of Hurricane squadrons stood at seventeen. And while not all of these squadrons were as yet operational the overall picture was made rather more heartening thanks to an emerging technology (RDF/radar) that would help to secure a new factor in aerial defence, something which today we might term a 'force multiplier'.

At the time the Hurricane was being developed in 1935 the RAF possessed thirteen frontline squadrons equipped with Furies, Demons or Bulldogs – all biplanes with fixed-pitch wooden propellers and fixed undercarriages. Thus did the prototype Hurricane K5083, a monoplane fighter originally tendered to Specification F36/34, offer a step change in capability. Initially intended to carry four Vickers Mk.V machine guns in the forward fuselage and wings, the Air Ministry subsequently modified the specification resulting in the installation of an eight-gun battery – all Brownings and all within the wings. Powered by an early Rolls-Royce Merlin, K5083 first flew on 6 November 1935.

The first production Hurricane was L1547 and almost as soon as the new fighter entered service efforts were made to develop and improve it, amongst the first of which was the fitting of a ventral strake under the rear fuselage when it became obvious that Hurricanes possessed poor spin recovery characteristics with the rudder becoming increasingly ineffective due to the breakdown of airflow under the lower fuselage. The situation was resolved by the RAE who established that the problem could be cured by adding a ventral strake under the rear section of fuselage and by extending the depth of the rudder, features that were introduced on the production line from the sixty-first airframe onwards.

The flight of the first production Hurricane, L1547 took place on 12 October 1937 and was powered by a 1,030hp Merlin II engine, with the type entering RAF service with 111 Squadron at Northolt, Middlesex, two months later. By the outbreak of war in Europe almost 500 Hurricanes had been produced, sufficient to equip seventeen frontline squadrons by late 1939. Whilst

manufacture of the first Hurricane order was underway the powerplant was switched from the Merlin II to the Merlin III from, approximately, the 360th airframe onwards. The Merlin II drove a Watts two-blade, fixed-pitch, wooden propeller that was inefficient at low airspeeds and required a long ground run to become airborne. Trials with a De Havilland two-pitch (coarse and fine) three-blade metal propeller demonstrated a significant reduction in the Hurricane's take-off run (from 1,230 to 750ft), and so the Merlin II was replaced by the Merlin III incorporating a 'universal' propeller shaft that allowed De Havilland and later types of propellers to be fitted.

Initially, the Hurricane's wing structure consisted of two steel spars with chordwise wooden formers which, like the tailplane, elevator, fin and rudder, was fabric covered – approximately 425 were

Above:
Prototype Hurricane K5083, then known as specification F.36/34 'High Speed Monoplane', is seen at Brooklands in November 1935 during its initial flight trials. Finished in an overall 'silver' scheme of highly polished metal engine panels and Aluminium doped fabric surfaces, it had standard 25 inch diameter Red/White/Blue fuselage roundels, with 49 inch diameter upperwing roundels and 45 inch underwing roundels. The serial number on the rear fuselage was 8 inches high in Night. No serials were carried under the wings at this time. Used for development purposes until production Hurricanes became available, K5083 became instructional airframe 1211M on 14 January 1939. Returned to the manufacturer, this important aircraft survived into 1942 after which, presumably, it was scrapped as there doesn't appear to be any record of its ultimate fate.

Below:
The first production Hurricane I, L1547, as seen in October 1937. Finished in the then newly adopted camouflage scheme of Dark Earth and Dark Green upper surfaces, to the A Scheme pattern, with Aluminium dope under surfaces and fuselage serial numbers incorrectly applied using 6 inch high characters instead of the official 8 inches, an anomaly that affected initial batches of Hurricanes until it was rectified on later airframes. Individual serial number characters on the wing under surfaces measured 30 inches from top to bottom and read from the front under the port wing and from the rear under the starboard wing. All serial numbers were in Night. Counterproductively, the standard Red/White/Blue roundels were outlined in Yellow on the wing upper surfaces and fuselage sides using a 1-3-5-7 ratio to make them more visible against the camouflage. Roundels measured 49 inches in diameter on the upper wing, 45 inches on the under surfaces, and 35 inches in diameter on the fuselage. *Carl Vincent*

Top right:
A full-frontal view of L1547 displaying its eight .303 Browning machine guns closely grouped in two batteries of four. It is easy nowadays to dismiss these weapons when considering, if considered at all, their relevance compared to later generation fighters equipped with 20mm cannon or .5in-calibre heavy machine guns. In 1937, eight harmonised rifle-calibre machine guns presented a truly withering armament – assuming a supply of good quality ammunition of course! Following trials with the manufacturers and the A&AEE, L1547 was later allocated to 312 Squadron but crashed on 10 October 1940 following an engine fire over the Mersey.

Bottom right:
A line of 111 Squadron Hurricane Is at Northolt in early 1938, each finished in the recently introduced Temperate Land Scheme with Yellow outlined roundels; identifiable are L1550 and L1566 – second and third from the camera respectively. This was the first operational unit to be equipped with the new fighter and as can be seen, unit markings have yet to be applied. All are fitted with Watts two-blade propellers, original 'kidney' exhaust manifolds, unarmoured windscreens, fuselage mounted instrument venturis (instead of underwing pitot tubes) and each lacks a ventral strake beneath the rudder. Of the two identifiable Hurricanes, L1550 bellylanded on 14 July 1938 and was DBR, while L1566 was written off at Sutton Bridge while being operated by 73 Squadron in May 1939.

so fitted. In April 1939, an all-metal wing covered with a stressed duralumin skin was designed which permitted a diving speed almost 80 mph faster than the earlier fabric-covered wing. Introduced in the second production batch from circa N2328, all subsequent Hurricanes were fitted with the new wings. Although fabric-wing Hurricanes still remained operational in mid-1940, most of the survivors had had them replaced retrospectively during servicing or repairs. It is worth noting that the one small advantage of a fabric wing was that bullets and cannon shells would often pass right through without exploding and, even if part of the internal structure was damaged, the repair was relatively simple and could be carried out by squadron groundcrew.

Further alterations were as follows: the first Hurricanes were fitted with so-called 'kidney-shaped' exhaust manifolds but these were soon superseded by three

manifold 'ejector' exhausts which were also retrofitted to the earlier airframes from mid to late 1938: early Hurricanes had a fork-pronged pitot under the port wing, this being gradually replaced by a single tube pitot over time: the original five-indent mainwheel hubs were reduced to four-indent hubs on later machines: early Hurricanes didn't have an additional access panel on the starboard mid-fuselage side as was fitted to all subsequent production machines to provide ground crews with easier access to the radio and associated equipment in the fuselage.

Pre-war Hawker Hurricane production batches
600 Hurricane Is completed by Hawker Aircraft between December 1937 and October 1939 in sequential serial range **L1547 to L2146** – as such these became the principal examples relevant to this

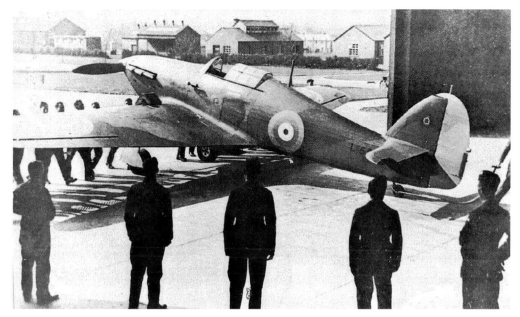

Left:
Hurricane I, L1555 of 111 Squadron at Northolt with possibly one of the earliest fittings of ejector exhausts as opposed to the more common kidney-type fitted to most early Hurricanes during this period. L1555 soon became the CO's aircraft. Later allocated to 6 OTU followed by 56 OTU, L1555 came to grief when it ran out of fuel and belly-landed in Norfolk on 17 April 1941 and was deemed to be DBR. *Tony O'Toole*

Below:
03-08-ST
Displaying 111 Squadron's badge on its fin, this early but unidentified Hurricane shows its 'kidney-shaped' exhaust manifolds, two-bladed wooden propeller, lack of ventral strake and 35 inch diameter Red/White/Blue/Yellow roundel on the fuselage. Also noticeable is the five-indent mainwheel hub, another characteristic of the early Hurricane. Flying overhead is Handley Page Harrow II, K7009, coded 'Z-214' of 214 Squadron – a type that will be covered in the next volume 'Before the Storm Vol 2: RAF Bombers 1930 - 1939'. *Tony O'Toole*

book.* However, additional Hurricane orders had been earlier placed with deliveries commencing in late 1939 as follows:

300 Mk.Is in <u>non</u>-sequential serial range **N2318 to N2729** (deliveries commenced September 1939 and completed in 1940). 1000 Mk.Is in <u>non</u>-sequential serial range **P2535 to P3984** (deliveries commenced November 1939 and completed by mid-1940).

* *It is instructive to realise that by 3 September 1939, between 495 and 500 Hurricanes had been completed with the majority going to the RAF; however, since entering service, peacetime Hurricane losses amounted to no less than seventy-nine, either destroyed outright, DBR, or permanently grounded and relegated to instructional airframe status. These figures do not include Hurricanes retained by the manufacturer, RAE or Rolls-Royce etc for development purposes, nor L1652 which crashed prior to delivery on 6 September 1938.*

Moreover, further to the losses mentioned and considering the rising tensions in Europe, it is perhaps surprising to note that dozens of Hurricanes from the first serial range were supplied to other air forces in 1938 and 1939 as shown in the list below.
L1918 - L1920, L1993 - L1997, L2040 - L2044, L2105 - L2111 – to Belgium

Top right:
The first frontline squadron to re-equip with the Hurricane, 111 Squadron was based at Northolt, Middlesex, which gradually relinquished its Gauntlets between December 1937 and February 1938. This image perfectly illustrates the two upper surface camouflage schemes applied to Hurricanes as the type entered service with L1550 in the foreground wearing the B Scheme camouflage whereas L1559 is in the A Scheme; both aircraft have 6 inch high fuselage serial numbers. The squadron badge in a standard frame is carried on the fins of both aircraft. As previously mentioned, L1550 met its end in July 1938, while L1559 became 1359M following a forced landing in Surrey on 17 January 1939.

L1759 - L1763, L1878 - L1888, L1890, L2021 - L2023 – to Canada. (L1848 sent as a pattern aircraft: L2144 sent but not received)
L2079 – to Iran
L2077, L2078, L2085, L2093 - L2097, L2104, L2112 - L2114 – to Romania
L1708, L1710, L1711, L1874 - L1876, L1909 – all diverted to the SAAF.
L2015 - L2017, L2019, L2024, L2025 L2027 - L2033, L2125 - L2139 – to Turkey
L1751, L1752, L1837 - L1840, L1858 - L1863 – to Yugoslavia
Further Hurricane deliveries from

subsequent serial batches continued in 1940, but they remain outside the scope of this volume.

Pre-war Supermarine Spitfire production batches
310 Spitfire Is completed by Supermarine, Woolston (213 delivered between July 1938 and June 1939 in sequential serial range **K9787 to K9999**: 97 in sequential serial range **L1000 to L1096** delivered between June and September 1939.)*
The next order covered **200** Mk.Is which were completed between September 1939

Bottom right:
Eleven 111 Squadron Hurricanes line up at Northolt in mid-1938. The CO's aircraft is fourth from the camera with full white numerals and Squadron Leader's pennant, whilst all the others have the tops of the numerals painted in red or blue to denote their respective Flights.

Top left:
Probably photographed
during a pre-delivery test
flight in 1938, L1582
obligingly shows the
upper surface B Scheme
camouflage pattern and
the Yellow outlined
upperwing roundels. Of
note is the way the Dark
Green areas had been
previously delineated
resulting in a slightly
darker outline while the
fairing between the
starboard wing and
centre section appears
to have retained its grey
primer. L1582 served
with both 3 and 73
Squadrons but was DBR
at Digby on 4 August
1939 after it stalled and
tipped on its nose.

and January 1940 within the non-sequential serial range **N3023 to N3299**. A further Spitfire I order was placed late in 1939 for 183 Mk.Is within non-sequential serial range **P9305 to P9567**, these are tenuously included given the date of the order: their delivery commenced in January 1940.
* *By 3 September 1939 all K9787 serial range Spitfires had been delivered as had most within the L1000 range. Although none of the latter appear to have been SOC prior to this date, thirty-seven K series Spitfires had been – either destroyed outright, DBR, cannibalised or relegated to instructional airframe status. Unlike the Hurricane, pre-war foreign orders for Spitfires were not fulfilled there being insufficient for the RAF and by the time production increased the war had long since commenced.*

The Spitfire was destined to become the backbone of Britain's air defence as well as becoming the most iconic fighter

ever produced by Britain's aero industries. However, given that the Spitfire's protracted development history is so well documented there is no need to repeat it here, suffice it to say that prototype K5054 made its first flight in March 1936, while the first production airframe, K9787, made its first flight on 15 May 1938, with K9789 becoming the first of its type to join an operational unit, namely 19 Squadron, on 4 August 1938. Disregarding a few cannon-armed Spitfires issued to 19 Squadron in 1940, plus a few used in developing photo-reconnaissance variants, all Mk.I Spitfires carried eight Browning machine guns distributed along the length of their wings as opposed to the two concentrated four-gun batteries carried by the Hurricane I.

Prior to the seventy-ninth production airframe, Spitfires were fitted with the Merlin II driving a two-blade wooden propeller, thereafter the Merlin III was fitted driving a De Havilland two-pitch (coarse and fine) three-blade metal propeller.

As with the Hurricane, Spitfires also underwent a programme of improvements virtually from the outset that included the replacement of the original flat-topped canopy hood with a domed hood to provide the pilot with more headroom, as well as an oval-shaped punch-out panel designed to equalise the pressure inside the cockpit in an emergency. The manually operated undercarriage retraction pump (which often caused the aircraft to 'porpoise' following take off) was replaced on the production line, from or about the 175th airframe, by a hydraulic pump located in the engine bay which was fitted retrospectively to earlier surviving airframes.

Initially, no armour plate was fitted to the back of the pilot's seat or behind the padded headrest of the earliest Spitfires (or Hurricanes); however, following the

Bottom left:
A further view of L1582
showing the initial
production Night/White
scheme with just the
outer, fabric covered,
sections of the wing
being painted leaving
the remainder of the
undersides in
Aluminium. Underwing
Red/White/Blue
roundels are present
although they were not
supposed to be applied
to the Night/White
scheme – and neither
were the underwing
serial numbers!
However, such errors,
dutifully painted in
contrasting Night under
the White wing and
White under the Night
wing presents a superb
example of precisely
what the Air Ministry did
not intend.

Top right:
Providing another excellent view of the upper surface B Scheme camouflage pattern, L1648, rolls towards the camera and also reveals it was fitted with the improved three manifold ejector exhausts which became standard. Again, the wing/centre section gap fairings appear to be painted in grey primer. Allocated to 85 Squadron, L1648 became another early loss and was DBR after it overshot while landing at Debden on 6 October 1938. *Tony Buttler*

Bottom right:
Hurricane I, L1583 belonging to 111 Squadron catches the light in such a way as to reveal the 'corrugated' effect of the early fabric covered wings. After serving in turn with 111, 263, 3 and 504 Squadrons, L1583 was SOC on 22 December 1941 while serving with the Air Transport Auxiliary. *Tony O'Toole*

Possibly taken at Hawker's Langley facility in Slough, factory fresh Hurricane I, L1791 is seen prior to taking to the air. Worthy of comment, beyond the fact that the underside of the White-painted wing features both a roundel and serial number, is the three-blade metal De Havilland propeller, metal-wings and manifold ejector exhausts – probably making L1791 among the very first Hurricanes to feature these modifications. Although the date of this photo is unknown, it is known that the Miles Magister I in the background (N541?) was delivered to the RAF between February and March 1939. Later allocated to 46 Squadron, followed by 7 OTU, L1791 bellylanded after losing power on 25 July 1940 and subsequently became instructional airframe 2172M.

outbreak of war, both types had headrest armour fitted at squadron or maintenance unit level from around February 1940, with armour behind the seat being provided from May of that year. Once the first 150 armour plate sets became available, orders were issued that 11 Group airfields were to be given priority.

Unlike early Hurricanes, Spitfires were fitted with three manifold ejector exhausts from the outset whereas, like the Hurricane, the original fork-pronged pitot tube was replaced by a single-tube pitot from mid-1939. By the beginning of 1939 the Spitfire's spin recovery parachute guard fitted to the top of the fin on some airframes had either been removed or was simply not fitted at all and, as with the Hurricane, Spitfires operated with unarmoured windscreens well into the summer of 1939 and both types retained ring and bead gunsights.

While the focus of this book ends in December 1939, it is instructive to consider further advances in propeller design that were literally just weeks away and were largely in effect by the beginning of the Battle of Britain and thereafter.

As mentioned, the wooden propellers had been replaced by metal two-pitch DH propellers which in turn were surpassed by a Rotol (**RO**lls/Bris**TOL**) constant-speed propeller unit (CSU). Developed early in 1940, the hydraulically operated CSU drove Jablo compressed-wood blades and were beginning to be fitted to Hurricanes from around the time of the Battle of France. Such was the transformation of Hurricane (and Spitfire) performance, De Havilland was prompted

Bottom left:
Seen at Leconfield in late 1938 or early 1939, this grainy image of an early unidentified Hurricane reveals (just) 73 Squadron's Medium Sea Grey 'HV-X' codes with a toned down modified fuselage roundel. The upperwing roundels would also have been modified to the Red/Blue style.

Top right:
Believed to be L1775 from 85 Squadron displaying the unit's pre-war code 'NO'. This Hurricane displays the ventral strake as fitted to later production aircraft. Also noticeable is the lighter coloured area beneath the starboard wing where the underwing roundel was painted out. L1775 was lost in France in May 1940. *Courtesy of Dave Welsh*

Centre and lower right:
Port and starboard views of an early production Hurricane that is believed to be L1634 which crashed after its engine cut while departing Debden, its home airfield. L1634 struck a ditch and overturned on 20 December 1938 and became instructional airframe 1358M as a consequence. It looks as if the aircraft was painted in the full Night/White scheme divided centrally along the fuselage centre line with just a red/blue roundel under the port (Night) wing and either side of the fuselage. While this aircraft was fitted with ejector exhausts, it still has a fork-prong style pitot under the port wing. The pre-war code 'NO' was allocated to 85 Squadron, the letter 'L' being L1634's individual code.

Left:
The wreck of 87 Squadron Hurricane L1629 following a fatal crash caused when a panel fell off in flight on 2 February 1939 near Debden, their home base. Just discernible is the 'ghost' of a serial number beneath the overpainted wing, this fighter having received the official Night/White scheme divided along the aircraft's centreline. Believe it or not, the modified roundels consist only of Blue and Red, however, the use of orthochromatic film has caused the Blue (outer) portion of the underwing roundel to appear very light indeed; equally, despite appearances to the contrary, the Yellow outer ring of the fuselage roundel had also been overpainted.

to undertake a programme of modifying their older two-pitch propellers into a similar CSU device. In June 1940, De Havilland began manufacturing a kit to convert their two-pitch propellers into constant speed propellers. Despite being heavier than the earlier type (500lb compared with 350lb), it provided a substantial improvement in climb rate while also reducing take-off distances. Commencing 24 June 1940, DII engineers

began fitting all Spitfires with these units and by 16 August virtually every operational *front-line* Spitfire and Hurricane had been modified (it would take longer to convert those in use with training or subsidiary units.)

Incremental weight increases changes had led to the Spitfire I, by mid-1940, attaining a lower maximum speed than they had in their original form, albeit effectively offset by the considerable

Above:
An intriguing photograph of 501 Squadron Hurricane 'SD-B', L2052, minus its engine and outer wing sections while undergoing maintenance or damage repair. This image was taken after the outbreak of war but prior to the re-application of Red/White/Blue fuselage roundels and before the unit was sent to France. L2052 displays the unit's code 'SD' (previously 'ZH') which was applied from September 1939 and retained until mid-1941. Also of note are the 6 inch high serial numbers, unarmoured windscreen and Aluminium under surfaces. It is tempting to suggest that the wings in the background might have belonged to Hurricane I L2062 and were about to be fitted to L2052 although we have no proof of this. L2052 was subsequently operated by several units and survived until April 1945, whereas L2062, if indeed that is what it is, was shot down on 1 September 1940 while serving with 32 Squadron.

Above:
Head-on view showing the Night/White/Aluminium under surface finish demarcation erroneously applied by Hawkers on the production line and some service units. What Dowding and the Air Ministry had actually intended was just a Night/White finish divided centrally down the aircraft's centreline. In this example at least, no underwing serials or roundels have been applied.
Tony Buttler

improvements gained in both take-off distance and rate of climb – essential elements for interceptors, where time to altitude was of utmost importance.

By the time the Battle of Britain was being fought the CSU-equipped Spitfire I had a maximum speed of around 353 mph at 20,000ft, however, once supplies of 100 octane fuel became available via the USA from early 1940, it made possible the use of an emergency boost of +12lb per square inch for almost five minutes, boosting the Merlin III's power rating of 1,030hp to 1,310hp at 3,000rpm at 9,000ft and increasing maximum speed by 25 mph at sea level and 34 mph at 10,000ft – as well as further improving climb performance. By the summer of 1940, almost all frontline Hurricanes and Spitfires were fitted with either a Rotol or De Havilland CSU.

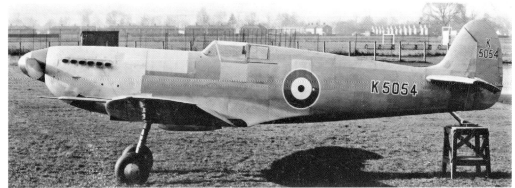

Below:
K5054 made its first flight on 5 March 1936 powered by a prototype Merlin C of 990hp driving a wooden two-bladed fixed-pitch propeller, it flew with its undercarriage fixed down and minus undercarriage doors with the airframe itself in unpainted condition. Following a number of early flights, the opportunity was taken to fit undercarriage doors and replace the tailskid with a tailwheel. Originally unarmed, the wings were later replaced with a pair incorporating eight .303in Browning machine guns. Seen here with its original engine exhausts, on 19 September 1937, K5054 was later fitted with new ejector exhaust manifolds developed by Rolls-Royce which, it was found, developed an additional 70lb of thrust – equivalent to about 70hp at 300 mph. K5054 came to grief on 4th September 1939 while being tested at Farnborough when the aircraft bounced and tipped over trapping the pilot who sustained serious neck injuries and died four days later.

At some point following its first flights, the prototype was returned to the factory and re-appeared a week or so later in an overall high-gloss, pale blue-grey finish applied by Rolls-Royce car factory personnel using automotive nitrocellulose lacquer, although there is continuing uncertainty over the actual colour or shade itself. The national markings (roundels) and the fuselage and rudder serial numbers appear to be identical to those carried when the K5054 was in its original unpainted state, that is: approximately 6 inch high Night serial numbers on the fuselage with approximately 4 inch high Night serial numbers on the rudder all outlined in White. By summer 1937, 12 inch high Night serial numbers had been applied to the wing under surfaces reading from the front beneath the port wing and from the rear under the starboard wing. 56 inch diameter Red/White/Blue/Yellow roundels were carried above the wings, with 35 inch diameter Red/White/Blue/Yellow roundels on the fuselage sides and 50 inch Red/White/Blue roundels under the wings. As flight trials continued the pale blue-grey finish deteriorated, possibly because the paint had been developed for cars rather than aircraft and was replaced by the RAF's then current Dark Earth and Dark Green scheme (to the A Scheme pattern) with Aluminium under surfaces which it carried for the rest of its service life.

Above:
Seen at Sea Island, British Columbia, in spring 1939, this photograph of a Hurricane I is unusual inasmuch that it shows its flaps in the fully down position, something not commonly photographed. Given the serial number 313, this and four other Hurricanes were delivered from RAF stocks in the serial range L1759 to L1763 to become RCAF 310 to 314. Were they renumbered in direct sequence? If so, then L1762 would have become 313. *Carl Vincent*

Centre left:
K5054, the prototype Spitfire as seen in unpainted condition, quite possibly prior to its first flight.

Top right:
K9787, the first production Spitfire I seen in full high-visibility Red/White/Blue/Yellow roundels on the wing upper surfaces and fuselage sides. Finished in the A Scheme, as befits the first airframe on the production line, its serial number has been applied to the rear fuselage and, unusually for Spitfires, on the rudder too. Other features of note are the unarmoured windscreen, 'flat-topped' canopy hood, pole aerial mast and spin recovery parachute guard at the top of the fin – all features of early production Spitfires. Later converted to the photo-reconnaissance role, K9787 was reported missing on 30 June 1941.
Tony Buttler

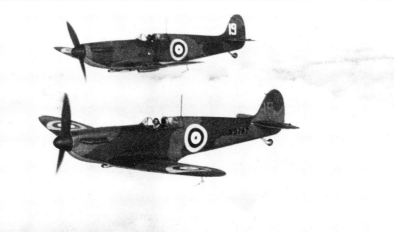

Centre right:
The first squadron to receive Spitfires was 19 Squadron in August 1938, just before the Munich Crisis. Spitfires were being delivered very slowly at the time, but on 8 October, still wearing pre-Munich high visibility roundels, six of the unit's aircraft attended a display for the opening of Cambridge Airport which was used as a publicity opportunity to photograph the new type for which the numeral '19' was applied to their fins. It is thought that all the aircraft had white '19's applied with the exception of K9797 – the CO's aircraft, Sqn Ldr Henry Cozens, which had a red '19' applied (seen here in the centre). Apparently, the fin markings only lasted a few days at most before being removed. The Spitfire in the foreground, K9794, in B Scheme camouflage, appears to have a domed canopy hood, surely one of the first Spitfires so fitted. All three still retain spin recovery parachute guards fitted at the top of the fin. Received by 19 Squadron on 4 October 1938, K9794 hit a fence at Digby on 10 January 1939 which caused its undercarriage to collapse on landing and was declared DBR.

Bottom right:
Spitfire I, K9795, was delivered to 19 Squadron on 27 September 1938 and remained with the unit long enough to eventually receive the code 'WZ-B'. The clarity of this photo is sufficient to be able to identify the widely spaced gun ports along the left wing's leading edge with flash eliminators for the outer pair and the spin recovery parachute guard fitted to the top of the fin. K9795 later served with 64 Squadron and was brought down by anti-aircraft fire over Dover on 18 April 1940. It survived the bellylanding and was duly repaired and returned to operational service prior to joining 58 OTU. K9795 was eventually SOC in January 1943.

Top left:
A somewhat blurred image of K9796, with white '19' applied to the fin and being an even-numbered serial it's likely the camouflage pattern would have been in the B Scheme. At this time, Spitfire under surfaces were still Aluminium with tiny 12 inch serial numbers – a restriction caused by a lack of space between the roundel and the mainwheel well. Despite appearances the fuselage roundel does include a Yellow outer ring. K9796 served with 19 Squadron from 3 October 1938 until November 1939, following which it served with a miscellany of non-operational units until finally SOC in April 1945, by which time very few Mk.I Spitfires remained. That said, apparently five Mk.Is did indeed remain on RAF 'books' in September 1945: were any still airworthy? One wonders. *Tony O'Toole*

Centre left:
Spitfire I, K9787, shows its upper surface A Scheme camouflage pattern and 56 inch diameter upperwing roundels. This aircraft was never allocated to a fighter squadron and after spending time with the A&AEE and RAE it was converted into a photo reconnaissance PR.I serving with 1 Photographic Reconnaissance Unit (1 PRU) until it went missing on 30 June 1941. *Tony Buttler*

Bottom left:
Photographed at Sutton Bridge on 6 February 1939, K9851 from 19 Squadron reveals that its under surfaces were still in the process of being painted in Night/White, with the under surfaces of the starboard wing appearing to have been painted white, while the under surfaces of the port wing still appear to be in Aluminium. Because of this the small black 12 inch high serial number remains clearly visible while the adjacent roundel has been overpainted in black (Night). The underside of the nose and rear fuselage also appear to be in Aluminium. The A scheme upper surface camouflage features the lower upper/under demarcation line on the engine cowling which was standard on early Spitfires. After serving with 19 Squadron, K9851 saw service with 7 and 57 OTU before being SOC on 1 August 1941.

Top right:
A well-known photograph of 65 Squadron Spitfire Is taken in the summer of 1939, one worthy of reproduction for the detail it offers. The aircraft in the foreground with the squadron's pre-war code 'FZ-L' is K9906, purportedly being flown by F/O Robert Stanford Tuck (as he then was and who would later achieve twenty-seven aerial victories plus two shared in battle). Although overpainted, the serial number K9906 remains barely discernible on the rear fuselage but does appear in miniature on the fin. Freshly applied areas of Dark Earth and Dark Green are apparent around the fuselage roundel, by now modified from 35 to 25 inches in diameter in Red/Blue in lieu of the previous Red/White/Blue/Yellow style. 'FZ-L' 'FZ-O' and 'FZ-P' all appear to wear Aluminium under surfaces, whereas 'FZ-A' 'FZ-H' and 'FZ-B' have had their port wing under surfaces painted in Night, with each divided down the centreline as the undersides of the noses and fuselages are in Night too. The upper/under surface demarcation on the noses of all the aircraft is in the lower position, generally following the curve of the cowling under surface contours rather than the straight panel line as on later Spitfires. All have de Havilland metal propellers and spinners and all have domed canopy hoods with the oval punch-out panel which was designed to equalise air pressure inside the cockpit in an emergency. K9906 was received by 65 Squadron on 24 March 1939, later becoming 'YT-T' with 64 Squadron on 17 April 1940. Ultimately the airframe went to 759 Squadron FAA in late 1943. (The white 'blobs' on the wing leading edge were a crude attempt by the censor to obscure the number of guns carried.)

Above:
Early 1940 and 616 Squadron display their Spitfire Is and their unit code 'QJ', the code having first been applied to Gauntlet IIs in September 1939 and then progressively transferred to Spitfires as they began to receive the latter in October – the last Gauntlets being finally disposed of in December 1939. (Fairey Battles were used temporarily to assist with the transition from fixed undercarriage open cockpit biplanes to the new fighter). 'QJ' was retained until October 1941 by which point 616 had been flying the Spitfire IIa for several months. The national markings seen here conformed to the earlier changes with Red/White/Blue roundels on the fuselage sides.

Bristol Blenheim If

Often overlooked, one other monoplane fighter entered operational service with the RAF prior to WWII. The Bristol Blenheim Mk.If was an adaptation of the famous Blenheim I twin-engined light bomber, the first production examples of which had reached RAF squadrons in March 1937 and created an immediate stir as, once again, a service bomber proved to be faster than the RAF's latest fighters; namely the Gauntlet and Gladiator. Requiring little in the way of alteration, approximately 200 Blenheim Is were converted from bombers by RAF maintenance units using conversion kits supplied by the Southern Railway's Ashford factory to thus become the Mk.If fighter, the first examples of which were received by 25 Squadron in October 1938 with 23, 29 and 64 Squadrons following in the same month. Training roles aside, the

Blenheim If would see use as an intruder, bomber escort, as a Coastal Command long-range maritime reconnaissance fighter and as a night fighter. Ultimately it would pioneer the use of airborne radar and, on 22/23 July 1940, it was a Blenheim fighter that scored the world's first combat victory using airborne radar.

By the end of 1939, twenty squadrons had or were receiving the fighter, while 600 Squadron had also begun to receive the Blenheim IVf, a lengthened variant of the Mk.If. Both types were fitted with a four-gun ventral gun tray containing four .303 Browning machine guns located over the now sealed bomb bay. Both fighter versions retained the single fixed Browning located in the port wing plus a single drum-fed .303 Vickers 'K' machine gun in the dorsal turret, both being standard on Blenheim bombers at this time.

Above:
As stated, no Blenheim fighters were built as such on the production line, but that was where their lives commenced. This view of Bristol's Filton factory was taken in 1938 or early 1939 when 450 Blenheim Is serialed L1097 to L1546 were under construction. L1164, whose fin and rudder is seen in the foreground, was originally delivered to 18 Squadron, a bomber unit, but was soon transferred and, following modification, was delivered to Hendon-based 600 Squadron – a fighter unit which in November 1939 would become the first to receive the Blenheim IVf. L1164 dived into the ground on approach to Hendon on 3 September 1939 – the very first day of the war.

Left:
By the start of 1940, Spitfire production was getting into its stride and factories were catching up with the marking changes. P9450, a Supermarine-built machine, produced in April 1940, is finished in the A Scheme, and had 35 inch Red/White/Blue fuselage roundels and 56 inch diameter Red/Blue upper surface wing roundels applied on the production line. The under surfaces of the wings were Night and White with nose, fuselage and tailplanes still in Aluminium. Underwing roundels were no longer applied to fighters by this time. P9450 was issued to 64 Squadron and was reported missing on 5 December 1940. *Tony Buttler*

Top right:
Unidentified Blenheim If 'RX-M' of 25 Squadron photographed c. August 1939. The fuselage and wing upper surface roundels have been modified into the post-Munich toned-down Red/Blue style by overpainting the Yellow outer ring as demonstrated by the fresher Dark Earth/Dark Green areas on the wing upper surfaces and enlarging the Red and Blue rings to cover the White. The code 'RX-M' is in Medium Sea Grey and the aircraft also carries the Fighter Spearhead on the fin with the squadron's hawk on a gauntlet motif, both of which disappeared after 3 September. It is thought that the under surface of the starboard wing and tailplane were painted white, with the exception of the aileron and elevator, with the rest of the under surfaces remaining in the original Night. The code 'RX' was allocated to 25 Squadron c. December 1938 and replaced by 'ZK' In September 1939. *Tony O'Toole*

Centre right:
Displaying their pre-war code 'YN' (changed to 'UF' in September 1939), four unidentified Blenheim If fighters from 601 Squadron formate in 1939. Previously equipped with Gauntlets, Blenheim fighters were used from March 1939 until February 1940 when they were replaced by the Hurricane I. The upper surface roundels will likely have been modified and toned-down in the Red/Blue style and it appears that their starboard wing under surfaces have been painted white, while the starboard aileron on the aircraft in the foreground (and possibly on the others), still remain in Night as does the tailplane and elevator to reveal yet another variation on the Night/White Scheme.

Below:
This unidentified Blenheim If presents an interesting view of the Night/White scheme. Blenheims were delivered with overall Night undersurfaces, with fighter variants subsequently receiving a coat of White beneath the starboard wing, in this instance from the leading edge to the trailing edge and including a portion of the fuselage adjacent to it. Also note that the underside of the starboard engine cowling remains in Night as does the undercarriage door and the ventral gun tray.

Above:
Coded 'UF-D', this otherwise anonymous Blenheim If ended up on its nose in late 1939 or early 1940 while serving with 601 Squadron. This photo is useful because it reveals the Blenheim's B Scheme upper surface camouflage pattern to good effect as well as the modified 47½ inch Red/Blue upper wing roundels. The fuselage roundels have been modified to the Red/White/Blue style of 35 inch diameter, and the code letters are approximately 40 inches high in Medium Sea Grey. *Carl Vincent*

Below:
Following the outbreak of war most RAF squadrons had their identifying codes changed, with 25 Squadron replacing 'RX' with 'ZK' in September 1939. Believed to be Blenheim If L1233, this image dates from early 1940. L1233 initially served with 101 Squadron as a Blenheim I before briefly transferring to 248 Squadron for night defence duties in December 1939, by which point it had been modified to a Mk.If. A month or so later it was serving with 25 Squadron as 'ZK-I' and was probably still with the unit when Beaufighter Ifs arrived in September 1940. Ultimately L1233 went to 12 (Pilots) Advanced Flying Unit which boasted over 90 Blenheim Mks.I, IV and V on strength by May 1943, but ended its days by overshooting the runway at Spittlegate near Grantham a month later. When photographed L1233's fuselage roundel had been updated to the Red/White/Blue style with correctly applied Night/White under surfaces divided centrally down the fuselage. *Tony O'Toole*

Production denied – Monoplane fighters that also ran but failed to reach the finishing post!

The Hurricane and Spitfire have become legendary, ensuring that their names will live on in RAF annals for generations to come. However, it is worth recalling that several other monoplane fighter designs were forwarded to the Air Ministry for consideration, many of which never left the drawing board, but other contenders did make it into the air, at least half a dozen in fact – four of which are included here.

This page:
Two views of the private venture Vickers Type 279 Venom, PV0-10, as seen in 1936. Responding to Specification F.5/34, Vickers produced the Venom, a fighter designed to overcome the performance advantages enjoyed by the fast day-bombers of the period. Equipped with a 625hp Bristol Aquila radial engine which hinged for easy access and servicing, it was also fitted with eight Browning machine guns (300 rpg) before either the Hurricane or Spitfire. It was estimated that the Venom would achieve a maximum speed of 320 mph at 15,000ft. First flown on 17 June 1936 by Mutt Summers, it proved very manoeuvrable and at 312 mph almost as fast as predicted. However, for a variety of reasons including a lack of engine development potential in comparison with the new Rolls-Royce PV12 (Merlin) the Venom proceeded no further and was scrapped in 1939, its demise hastened by the large orders previously placed for the Hurricane and Spitfire. *Tony Buttler*

Above:
This aircraft has been likened by one present day U-Tube commentator as 'Britain's own Zero' of which, admittedly, there is something of a passing resemblance, but I digress. The Gloster Aircraft Company was awarded a contract to produce two prototype eight-gun fighters in response to Air Ministry Specification F5/34: the two prototypes receiving the serials K5604 and K8089 respectively. Both were powered by an 840hp Bristol Mercury IX radial engine driving a two-pitch three-blade De Havilland metal propeller with the first, K5604, flying in December 1937. The second one flew in March 1938, by which time it was fitted with eight Browning machine guns with 300 rpg. Given that by this time the higher performance Hurricane and Spitfire were already in production no further orders for the Gloster F5/34 were forthcoming. The Gloster F.5/34 had a maximum speed of 316 mph at 16,000ft and a service ceiling of 32,000ft. *Tony Buttler*

Left:
P9594, the Martin-Baker Aircraft company's M.B.2 interceptor, was another contender for an eight-gun fighter as per Specification F5/34. Fitted with a 1,000hp Napier Dagger III engine driving a wooden two-blade propeller the MB.2 achieved 305 mph at just under 10,000ft and featured a fixed 'trousered' undercarriage. No production orders ensued.
Tony Buttler

Below:
One of the more surprising fighter concepts existing in mid-1939 was this – one indicative of an urgent need to acquire fighters on the one hand or, and I speculate, a well-armed trainer that could be used to strafe enemy beachheads should/when an invasion of southern Britain be attempted. The Miles Master I was an advanced trainer powered by a 715hp Rolls-Royce Kestrel XXX engine armed with a single fixed .303 machine gun. However, of the many hundreds procured for the RAF twenty-four (or twenty-six) were configured in such a way that they could be quickly transformed into the Miles M.24 Emergency Fighter by removing the rear seat and a section of cockpit glazing and installing six .303in Brownings. The top speed of a Master I was 226 mph at 15,000ft, presumably a similar performance would have applied to the M.24 too; happily the question of how effective it might have been against the enemy remains a matter of conjecture as they were never called into action. N7412, seen here, was one of the M.24 Fighters that was fitted for, but never with the six guns mentioned. While serving with 9FTS, N7412 inexplicably dived into the ground on 23 July 1941. *Tony O'Toole collection*

Appendix 1: RAF: Fighter Squadrons and their aircraft 1930 to December 1939

KEY:
F = formed, RE = re-established, RF = re-formed, D = disbanded

Blank segments indicate non-fighter squadrons (to be covered in subsequent volumes)

Solid segments indicate that a given squadron had yet to form or reform. (Solid segments extending across entire decade denote squadrons formed/reformed post 1939 – with aircraft type indicated [where known] for additional interest.)

In-service dates. These often refer to the date when the first of a given type was received by a squadron and does not necessarily imply that a unit had received its full complement of aircraft, nor indeed that it was operational on type.

Out-of-service dates: it should not be assumed that the dates listed represent a type's final period of service; many aircraft, particularly obsolescing biplanes, commonly served in subsidiary roles for months or even years afterwards with some, on occasion, being temporarily returned to operational duties for want of anything else.

UNIT	c 1930 - 1936	1937	1938	1939	NOTES
1 Sqn RF 2.27	Siskin IIIA 2.27 - 2.32 Fury I 2.32	Fury I	Fury I to 11.38 Hurricane I 10.38	Hurricane I to 4.41	Gladiator I briefly 2.37 - 3.37
2 Sqn					
3 Sqn RF 4.24	Gamecock 8.28 - 7.29 Bulldog II/IIA 5.29	Bulldog IIA to 7.37 Gladiator I 3.37	Gladiator I to 3.38 Hurricane I 3.38 - 7.38 Gladiator I from 7.38	Gladiator I to 7.39 Hurricane I 5.39 - 4.41	
4 Sqn					
5 Sqn					
6 Sqn F 1.14	Bristol F.2B 7.20 - 6.32 Gordon 6.31 - 10.35 Demon 9.35 - 11.36 Hart 10.35	Hart	Hart to 1.38 Hardy 1.38	Hardy to 4.40 Gauntlet I, II 8.39-4.40 Lysanders from 9.39	Mid-East 1919. Demons D Flight only. 10 Gauntlets plus Lysanders and Hardys used for anti-slavery and aerial policing patrols in Palestine
7 Sqn					
8 Sqn					
9 Sqn					
10 Sqn					
11 Sqn					
12 Sqn					
13 Sqn					
14 Sqn					
15 Sqn					
16 Sqn					
17 Sqn RF 4.24	Gamecock 1.28 - 9.28 Siskin IIIA 9.28 - 10.29 Bulldog II/IIA 10.29-8.36 Gauntlet II 8.36	Gauntlet II	Gauntlet II	Gauntlet II to 6.39 Hurricane I 6.39 - 2.41	
18 Sqn					
19 Sqn RF 4.23	Siskin IIIA 3.28 - 9.31 Bulldog IIA 9.31 - 1.35 Gauntlet I 1.35 Gauntlet II 9.36	Gauntlet I Gauntlet II	Gauntlet I Gauntlet II Spitfire I 8.38	Gauntlet I to 3.39 Gauntlet II to 2.39 Spitfire I to 12.40	
20 Sqn					
21 Sqn					
22 Sqn					
23 Sqn RF 7.25	Gamecock 4.26 - 9.31 Bulldog IIA 7.31 - 3.33 Hart Fighter 7.31 -1935 Demon 7.33	Demon	Demon to 12.38 Blenheim If 12.38	Blenheim If to 4.41	Hart Fighters were the immediate predecessors to the Demon, at least two of which survived with 23 Sqn into 1935
24 Sqn					
25 Sqn RF 5.20	Siskin IIIA 3.29 - 3.32 Fury I 2.32 Fury II 11.36	Fury I into 1937 Fury II to 10.37 Demon 10.37	Demon to 6.38 Gladiator I 6.38 Blenheim If 12.38	Gladiator I to 2.39 Blenheim If to 1.41	
26 Sqn					
27 Sqn					
28 Sqn					
29 Sqn RF 4.23	Siskin IIIA 3.28 - 6.32 Bulldog IIA 6.32 - 4.35 Demon 3.35 - 8.36 Gordon 3.36 - 8.36 Demon (Turret) 10.36	Demon (Turret)	Demon (Turret) to 12.38 Blenheim If 12.38	Blenheim If to 2.41	Sqn sent to Egypt 10.35 re Abyssinia crisis: Gordons used for night patrol duties. Unit returned to UK mid-9.36

UNIT	c 1930 - 1936	1937	1938	1939	NOTES
30 Sqn					
31 Sqn					
32 Sqn RF 4.23	Gamecock　9.26 - 4.28 Siskin IIIA　4.28 - 1.31 Bulldog IIA　9.30 - 7.36 Gauntlet II　　7.36	Gauntlet II	Gauntlet II　to 10.38 Hurricane I　10.38	Hurricane I　to 7.41	
33 Sqn RF 3.29	Horsley II　3.29 - 5.30 Hart　　2.30	Hart	Hart　to 3.38 Gladiator I　2.38	Gladiator I　to 6.40	RF as day bomber sqn. M-East 10.35 Became a fighter sqn 3.38. Gauntlets rec'd 2.40 to conserve Gladiator hours were still available in 6.40
34 Sqn					
35 Sqn					
36 Sqn					
37 Sqn					
38 Sqn					
39 Sqn					
40 Sqn					
41 Sqn RF 4.23	Siskin IIIA　3.27 - 11.31 Bulldog IIA　10.31 - 8.34 Demon　　7.34	Demon　to 10.37 Fury II　10.37	Fury II	Fury II　to 1.39 Spitfire I　1.39 - 11.40	
42 Sqn					
43 Sqn RF 7.25	Gamecock　4.26 - 6.28 Siskin IIIA　6.28 - 5.31 Fury I　　5.31	Fury I	Fury I Hurricane I　12.38	Fury I　to 1.39 Hurricane I　to 4.41	
44 Sqn					
45 Sqn					
46 Sqn RF 9.36	Gauntlet II　　9.36	Gauntlet II	Gauntlet II	Gauntlet II　to 3.39 Hurricane I　3.39 - 5.41	
47 Sqn					
48 Sqn					
49 Sqn					
50 Sqn					
51 Sqn					
52 Sqn					
53 Sqn					
54 Sqn RF 1.30	Siskin III(DC) 1.30-12.30 Bulldog IIA　4.30 - 9.36 Gauntlet II　　8.36	Gauntlet II to 5.37 Gladiator I　4.37	Gladiator I	Gladiator I　to 4.39 Spitfire I　3.39 - 2.41	Siskin III(DC) = Dual Control trainer.
55 Sqn					
56 Sqn RF 11.22	Siskin IIIA　9.27 - 10.32 Bulldog IIA　10.32 - 5.36 Gauntlet II　　5.36	Gauntlet II to 7.37 Gladiator I　7.37	Gladiator I　to 5.38 Hurricane I　from 4.38	Hurricane I　to 2.41	
57 Sqn					
58 Sqn					
59 Sqn					
60 Sqn					
61 Sqn					
62 Sqn					
63 Sqn					
64 Sqn RF 3.36	Demon　　3.36	Demon	Demon　to 12.38 Blenheim If　12.38	Blenheim If　to 4.40	RF in Egypt, returned to UK in 9.36. (Re-equipped Spitfire I from 4.40)
65 Sqn RF 8.34	Demon　8.34 - 7.36 Gauntlet II　7.36	Gauntlet II to 6.37 Gladiator I　6.37	Gladiator I	Gladiator I　to 4.39 Spitfire I　3.39 - 4.41	
66 Sqn RF 7.36	Gauntlet II　7.36	Gauntlet II	Gauntlet II　to 12.38 Spitfire I　10.38	Spitfire I　to 11.40	
67 Sqn					RF 3.41 (Buffalo I)
68 Sqn					RF 1.41 (Blenheim I)
69 Sqn					RF 1.41 (Maryland I)
70 Sqn					
71 Sqn					RF in UK 9.40 (Buffalo I)
72 Sqn RF 2.37		Gladiator I　2.37	Gladiator I	Gladiator I　to 5.39 Spitfire I　4.39 - 4.41	Gladiators used 3.40 (Acklington being temporarily unserviceable for Spitfires for two weeks)

Appendix 1: RAF: Fighter Squadrons and their aircraft 1930 to December 1939
Continued

UNIT	c 1930 - 1936	1937	1938	1939	NOTES
73 Sqn RF 3.37		Fury II 3.37 - 7.37 Gladiator I 6.37	Gladiator I to 7.38 Hurricane I 7.38	Hurricane I to 1.42	To France 9.39
74 Sqn RF 9.35	Demon 9.35	Demon to 4.37 Gauntlet II 3.37	Gauntlet II	Gauntlet II .to 2.39 Spitfire I 2.39 - 9.40	Known as 'Demon Flights' to 11.35, 74 Sqn had reformed in 9.35 while en route Malta. Returned UK in 9.36
75 Sqn					
76 Sqn					
77 Sqn					
78 Sqn					
79 Sqn RF 3.37		Gauntlet II 3.37	Gauntlet II to 11.38 Hurricane I 11.38	Hurricane I to 4.41	
80 Sqn RF 3.37		Gauntlet II 3.37 - 5.37 Gladiator I 5.37	Gladiator I	Gladiator I to 11.40	To Egypt 5.38 for defence of Canal region. ('A' Flight rec'd Hurricanes 6.40: Gladiator IIs 11.40 to 3.41)
81 Sqn					
82 Sqn					
83 Sqn					
84 Sqn					
85 Sqn RF 6.38			Gladiator I 6.38- 9.38 Hurricane I 9.38	Hurricane I to 4.41	To France 9.39
86 Sqn					RF 12.40 (Blenheim IV)
87 Sqn RF 3.37		Fury II 3.37 - 6.37 Gladiator I - 6.37	Gladiator I to 8.38 Hurricane I from 7.38	Hurricane I to 9.42	To France 4.9.39
88 Sqn					
89 Sqn					RF 9.41 (Beaufighter If)
90 Sqn					
91 Sqn					RF 1.41 (Spitfire IIA)
92 Sqn RF 10.39				Blenheim If 10.39	Spitfire I replaced Blenheim If 3.40
93 Sqn RF 12.40					Night fighter unit. Rec'd Harrow II (LAM) and Havoc I
94 Sqn RF 3.39				Gladiator I 3.39 - 4.40 Gladiator II 3.39 - 6.41	RF Khormaksar as fighter defence for Aden
95 Sqn					
96 Sqn					RF 12.40 (Hurricane I)
97 Sqn					
98 Sqn					
99 Sqn					
100 Sqn					
101 Sqn					
102 Sqn					
103 Sqn					
104 Sqn					
105 Sqn					
106 Sqn					
107 Sqn					
108 Sqn					
109 Sqn					RF 12.40 (Whitley V)
110 Sqn					
111 Sqn RF 10.23	Siskin IIIA 9.26 - 2.31 Bulldog IIA 1.31 - 6.36 Gauntlet I/II 6.36	Gauntlet I/II Hurricane I 12.37	Gauntlet I/II to 2.38 Hurricane I	Hurricane I to 4.41	
112 Sqn RF 5.39				Gladiator I/II 6.39- 6.41	RF en route Egypt on HMS *Argus* with 24 crated Gladiators (Gauntlets rec'd 1939/40 with five active on 10.6.40)
113 Sqn					
114 Sqn					
115 Sqn					
116 Sqn to 138 Sqn inclusive all reformed post-1939					
139 Sqn					
140 Sqn					RF 9.41 (Spitfire C)
141 Sqn RF 10.39				Gladiator I 10.39 - 4.40 Blenheim If 11.39 -5.40	Both types used to train crews prior to arrival of Defiants (in 4.40)
142 Sqn					
143 Sqn					RF 6.41 (Beaufighter Ic)
144 Sqn					

UNIT	c 1930 - 1936	1937	1938	1939	NOTES
145 Sqn RF 10.39				Blenheim If 10.39- 5.40	RF as a fighter unit pending arrival of Hurricanes
146 Sqn					RF 10.41 (Audax 'fighter')
147 Sqn					RF 9.44 (Dakota)
148 Sqn					
149 Sqn					
150 Sqn					
151 Sqn RF 8.36	Gauntlet II 8.36	Gauntlet II	Gauntlet II Hurricane I 12.38	Gauntlet II to 3.39 Hurricane I to 6.41	
152 Sqn RF 10.39				Gladiator I/II 10.39-1.40 Spitfire I 12.39 - 3.41	
153 Sqn to 165 Sqn inclusive formed/reformed post-1939					
166 Sqn					
167 Sqn to 184 Sqn inclusive formed/reformed post-1939					
185 Sqn					
186 Sqn to 200 Sqn inclusive formed/reformed post-1939					
201 Sqn					
202 Sqn					
203 Sqn					
204 Sqn					
205 Sqn					
206 Sqn					
207 Sqn					
208 Sqn					
209 Sqn					
210 Sqn					
211 Sqn					
212 Sqn					RF Meaux, France 2.40. (Spitfire 'C')
213 Sqn RF 3.37		Gauntlet II 3.37	Gauntlet II	Gauntlet II to 3.39 Hurricane I 1.39 - 3.42	
214 Sqn					
215 Sqn					
216 Sqn					
217 Sqn					
218 Sqn					
219 Sqn RF 10.39				Blenheim If 10.39 -2.41	RF to protect east coast shipping, becoming operational 21.2.40
220 Sqn					
221 Sqn					RF 11.40 (Wellington IC)
222 Sqn RF 10.39				Blenheim If 10.39 -3.40	RF as shipping protection unit. Role changed 3.40 with arrival of Spitfire I
223 Sqn					
224 Sqn					
225 Sqn					
226 Sqn					
227 Sqn					RF 1942 (Beaufighter Ic)
228 Sqn					
229 Sqn RF 10.39				Blenheim If 10.39 -3.40	RF for shipping protection and convoy patrol. Hurricane Is rec'd 3.40
230 Sqn					
231 Sqn					RF 7.40 (army co-op unit Lysander II)
232 Sqn					RF 7.40 (Hurricane I)
233 Sqn					
234 Sqn RF 10.39				Battle 11.39 - 3.40 Blenheim If 11.39 -3.40 Gauntlet II 11.39 -12.39	RF for shipping protection duties but role altered to day fighter sqn. Spitfire Is rec'd from 3.40
235 Sqn RF 10.39				Battle 10.39 - 2.40 (Training purposes only)	Blenheim If/IVf by 2.40. To C.C. 2.40 for convoy protection/recce duties
236 Sqn RF 10.39				Blenheim If 11.39 -7.40	Transferred to Coastal Command 29.2.40
237 Sqn					RF Kenya 4.40 (from 1 Sqn Southern Rhodesian AF on Audax, Hardy, Hart)
238 Sqn					RF 5.40 (Spitfire I)
239 Sqn					RF 9.40 (Lysander II)
240 Sqn					
241 Sqn					RF 9.40 (Lysander II)

Appendix 1: RAF: Fighter Squadrons and their aircraft 1930 to December 1939
Continued

UNIT	c 1930 - 1936	1937	1938	1939	NOTES
242 Sqn RF 10.39				Battle 10.39 - 2.40 Blenheim If 12.39 only	Reformed as a fighter sqn. (Hurricane Is received 2.40)
243 Sqn					RF 3.41 (Buffalo I)
244 Sqn					RF 11.40 (Vincent)
245 Sqn RF 10.39				Blenheim If 11.39- 3.40	Reformed as a fighter sqn. (Hurricane Is received 3.40)
246 Sqn					RF 8.42 (Sunderland III)
247 Sqn					RF 8.40 (Gladiator II)
248 Sqn RF 10.39				Blenheim If 12.39 -5.40	Reformed as night defence sqn with 18 Blenheims. To Coastal Command 2.40: rec'd Blenheim IVf
249 Sqn					RF 5.40 (Spitfire then Hurricane)
250 Sqn					RF 4.41 (Tomahawk IIB)
251 Sqn					RF 8.44 (Hudson III / Ventura I)
252 Sqn					RF 11.40 (Blenheim If)
253 Sqn RF 10.39				Battle 12.39 - 4.40 Anticipated Blenheim If but none delivered	Hurricane I by 2.40
254 Sqn RF 10.39				Blenheim If 11.39- 4.40	RF as shipping protection unit. (Later transferred to Coastal Command)
255 Sqn					RF 11.40 (Defiant I)
256 Sqn					RF 11.40 (Defiant I)
257 Sqn					RF 5.40 Spitfire I
258 Sqn					RF 11.40 (Hurricane I)
259 Sqn					RF 2.43 (Catalina IB)
260 Sqn					RF 11.40 (Hurricane I)
261 Sqn					F 8.40 (Sea Gladiator I, Hurricane I)
262 Sqn					F 9.42 (Catalina IB)
263 Sqn RF 10.39				Gladiator I/II 10.39-4.40	
264 Sqn RF 10.39				Defiant I 12.39 - 9.41	
265 Sqn					F 4.43 (Catalina IB)
266 Sqn RF 10.39				Battle 12.39 - 4.40	Originally expected Blenheim If, but none rec'd. Spitfire Is arrived 1.40
267 Sqn					RF 8.40 (Proctor I et al – Comms sqn)
268 Sqn					RF 9.40 (Lysander II)
269 Sqn					
270 Sqn					RF 11.42 (Catalina IB)
271 Sqn					RF 5.40 (HP 42 et al – Transport Sqn)
272 Sqn					RF 11.40 (Blenheim IVf)
273 Sqn					
274 Sqn					RF 8.40 (Gladiator II)

275 to 299 squadrons formed/reformed post-1939.

300 to 312 squadrons formed in 1940: later 300-series units formed from 1941.

400-series squadrons formed from 1941 onwards.

505 to 509 (plus 599) Squadron were never formed: later 500-series squadrons formed from 1942.

606 Squadron never formed

Please note:

The squadrons listed below commenced life as bomber units, but as the decade advanced and the threat to Britain altered their roles were subsequently adjusted to reflect this. Hence aircraft complements are shown in full to emphasise the changes made and when.

UNIT	c 1930 - 1936	1937	1938	1939	NOTES
500 Sqn F 3.31	Virginia X 1931 - 1936 Hart 1.36	Hart 5.37 Hind 2.37	Hind	Hind to 3.39 Anson 3.39 - 4.41	Night-, later a day-bomber sqn, then general reconnaissance in 11.38
501 Sqn F 6.29	DH.9A 3.30 - 11.30 Wapiti 9.30 - 3.33 Wallace I from 3.33 Wallace II 3.36 - 6.36 Hart from 7.36	Wallace I to 2.37 Hart	Hart to 3.38 Hind from 3.38	Hind to 3.39 Hurricane I 3.39 - 5.41	Formed as a day bomber unit. Redesignated as a fighter sqn 12.38
502 Sqn F 5.25	Vimy 6.25 - 7.28 Hyderabad 7.28 - 2.32 Virginia X 12.31 - 10.35 Wallace I/II 10.35	Wallace I/II 5.37 Hind 4.37	Hind	Hind to 4.39 Anson I 1.39 - 10.40	Night- then day-bomber unit. 502 Sqn converted to general reconnaissance role in 11.38. (Rec'd Blackburn Botha 8.40)
503 Sqn F 10.26	Fawn 1926 - 1929 Hyderabad 2.29 - 1.34 Hinaidi 10.33 - 11.35 Wallace I/II 10.35 - 9.36 Hart 6.36	Hart	Hart to 11.38 Hind 6.38 to 11.38		Became 616 Sqn 1.11.38

UNIT	c 1930 - 1936	1937	1938	1939	NOTES
504 Sqn F 3.28	Horsley 10.29 - 2.34 Wallace I 1.34 Wallace II 2.35	Wallace I to 6.37 Wallace II to 6.37 Hind from 5.37	Hind to 11.38 Gauntlet II by 11.38	Gauntlet II to 8.39 Hurricane I 5.39 - 7.41	Formed as a day bomber unit. Redesignated as a fighter sqn 10.38
600 Sqn F 10.25	DH.9A 10.25 - 10.29 Wapiti IIA 8.29 - 1.35 Hart 1.35	Hart to 4.37 Demon 2.37	Demon	Demon to 2.39 Blenheim If 1.39-10.41 Blenheim IVf 11.39- 6.40	Day bomber sqn. Role change to fighter sqn 7.34. (Wapitis retained pending arrival of Harts)
601 Sqn F 10.25	DH.9A 6.26 - 10.30 Wapiti IIA 11.29 - 6.33 Hart 2.33	Hart to 8.37 Demon 8.37	Demon to 12.38 Gauntlet II by 12.38	Gauntlet II to 3.39 Blenheim If 1.39 - 2.40	Day bomber sqn. Role change to fighter sqn 1.7.34. (Harts retained pending arrival of Demons)
602 Sqn F 9.25	DH.9A 10.25 - 1.28 Fawn 9.27 - 10.29 Wapiti IIA 7.29 - 4.34 Hart 2.34 - 6.36 Hind from 6.36	Hind	Hind to 11.38 Hector from 11.38	Hector to 1.39 Gauntlet II 1.39 - 5.39 Spitfire I 5.39 - 6.41	Day bomber unit to 10.38. Army co-op 1.11.38 to 14.1.39 Fighter sqn thereafter
603 Sqn F 10.25	DH.9A 10.25 - 5.30 Wapiti IIA 9.30 - 1934 Hart from 2.34	Hart	Hart to 2.38 Hind from 2.38	Hind to 3.39 Gladiator II 3.39 -10.39 Spitfire I 9.39 - 11.41	Day bomber unit. Became a fighter sqn 24.10.38 with Hinds pending arrival of Gladiators
604 Sqn Formed 3.30	DH.9A 4.30 - 10.30 Wapiti IIA 9.30 - 3.34 Hart 9.34 - 6.35 Demon 6.35	Demon	Demon	Demon to 1.39 Blenheim If 1.39 - 5.41	Day bomber unit. Redesignated as a fighter sqn on 27.3.34 awaiting Harts then Demons
605 Sqn F 10.26	DH.9A 10.26 - 7.30 Wapiti IIA 4.30 - 11.34 Hart 2.34 - 9.36 Hind 8.36	Hind	Hind	Hind to 1.39 Gladiator I 3.39 -11.39 Gladiator II 1939 Hurricane I 6.39 -12.40	Day bomber unit. Redesignated as fighter sqn 1.1.39.
606 Sqn					Number not taken up
607 Sqn F 3.30	Wapiti IIA 12.32 Demon 9.36	Wapiti IIA to 1.37 Demon	Demon Gladiator I 12.38	Demon to 4.39 (last disposed of by 8.39) Gladiator I to 5.40	Day bomber unit. Training only until Wapitis rec'd. Redesignated fighter sqn 23.9.36. France 11.39
608 Sqn F 3.30	Wapiti IIA 6.30	Wapiti IIA to 1.37 Demon 1.37	Demon	Demon to 3.39 Anson I 3.39 - 5.41	Day bomber unit. Became fighter sqn 16.1.37 to 20.3.39; then became a general reconnaissance unit
609 Sqn F 2.36	Hart 5.36	Hart	Hart to 1.38 Hind 1.38	Hind to 9.39 Spitfire I 8.39 - 5.41	Day bomber unit. Became fighter sqn on 8.12.38 retaining Hinds pending arrival of Spitfires in 8.39 and 9.39
610 Sqn F 2.36	Hart 5.36	Hart	Hart to 5.38 Hind 5.38	Hind to 9.39 Hurricane I 9.39 only Spitfire I 9.39 - 2.41	Day bomber unit. Fighter sqn 1.1.39. Defiants anticipated but Hurricanes rec'd – followed rapidly by Spitfires
611 Sqn F 2.36	Hart 6.36	Hart	Hart to 4.38 Hind 4.38	Hind to 5.39 Spitfire I 5.39 - 9.40	Day bomber unit. Fighter sqn 1.1.39 pending arrival of Spitfires
612 Sqn F 6.37		Hector 12.37	Hector	Hector to 11.39 Anson I 6.39 - 1.41	General reconnaissance unit from 1.11.38
613 Sqn F 3.39				Hind 4.39 - 4.40 Hector 11.39 - 7.40	Formed as an army co-op unit
614 Sqn F 6.37		Hind 6.37	Hind Hector 4.38	Hind to 1.39 Hector to 2.40 Lysander II 7.39 - 7.41	Formed as an army co-op unit
615 Sqn F 6.37		Audax 11.37 Hector 11.37	Audax to 3.38 Hector to 11.38 Gauntlet II 12.38	Gauntlet II to 9.39 Gladiator I 6.39 - 10.39 Gladiator II 10.39 - 5.40	Army co-op unit initially (Hectors retained to 2.39). 615 Sqn became a fighter unit on 7.11.38
616 Sqn F 11.38			Hind from 11.38	Gauntlet II 1.39 - 12.39 Battle 5.39 - 11.39 Spitfire I 10.39 - 2.41	503 Sqn redesignated 616 Sqn. Role changing from bomber to fighter unit with effect 1.11.38

Appendix 2: Basic technical data

AIRCRAFT NAME	POWERPLANT Mean hp only. Power varied with altitude & RPM etc.*	MAX SPEED at stated altitude: (1000ft = 304.8m)	SERVICE CEILING Imperial (metric)	WING SPAN Imperial (metric)	FUSELAGE LENGTH Imperial (metric)	ARMAMENT Imperial (metric)
Snipe	Bentley BR.2 rotary. 250hp	125 mph – sea level 121 mph c. 10,000ft	19,500ft (5943m)	31ft 1in (9.44m)	19ft 9in (6.01m)	2x .303 (7.7mm) Vickers mg. 4x 20lb (9kg) bombs
Grebe II	Armstrong Siddeley (A/S) Jaguar IV radial. c.400hp	161 mph – sea level 145 mph – 10,000ft	23,000ft (7010m)	29ft 4in (8.93m)	20ft 3in (6.17m)	2x .303 (7.7mm) Vickers mg (600 rpg)
Siskin III	A/S Jaguar III radial. c.325hp	134 mph – sea level 128 mph – 15,000ft	20,500ft (6248m)	33ft 1in (10.08m)	23ft 0in (7.01m)	2x .303 Vickers mg (600 rpg) 4x25lb (11kg) bombs
Woodcock II	Bristol Jupiter IV radial. 425hp	141 mph – sea level 115 mph – 20,000ft	22,500ft (6858m)	32ft 6in (9.9m)	26ft 2in (7.96m)	2x .303 Vickers mg (with unverified 750 rpg)
Gamecock	Bristol Jupiter VI (or VII ?) radial c.425hp	154 mph – sea level 145 mph – 10,000ft	22,100ft (6736m)	29ft 9½in (9.067m)	19ft 8in (5.99m)	2x .303 Vickers (600 rpg)
Siskin IIIA	A/S Jaguar IV – later IVA (supercharged) c.385-420hp	143 mph – sea level 153 mph – 10,000ft	27,000ft (8229m)	33ft 2in (10.11m)	25ft 4in (7.72m)	2x .303 Vickers 600 rpg + 4x 20lb (9kg) bombs
Bulldog II	Bristol Jupiter VII radial 425hp	174 mph – 10,000ft	29,300ft (8930m)	33ft 10in (10.33m)	25ft 2in (7.68m)	2x .303 Vickers 600 rpg + 4x 20lb (9kg) bombs
Bulldog IIA	Bristol Jupiter VIIF radial 440hp	178 mph – 10,000ft	29,300ft (8930m	33ft 10in (10.33m	25ft 2in (7.68m	IIA's auw = 170lb [77kg] greater than Bulldog II
Fury I	Rolls-Royce Kestrel IIS liquid cooled in-line c.525hp	207 mph – 14,000ft	28,000ft (8534m)	30ft 0in (9.14m)	26ft 8in (8.125m)	2x .303 Vickers Mk.II/III and V progressively (600 rpg)
Fury II	R-R Kestrel VI liquid cooled in-line. 640hp	223 mph – 16,500ft	29,500ft (8991m)	30ft 0in (9.14m)	26ft 9in (8.153m)	2x .303 Vickers Mk.V (600 rpg). Mk.II auw = 119lb (54kg) greater than Mk.I
Demon I	Kestrel IIS 581hp.	181 mph – 13,400ft 155 mph – 3,300ft	24,500ft (7467m)	37ft 3in (11.35m)	29ft 7in (8.993m)	2x Vickers III/V (600 rpg). 1x .303 Lewis gun (6 x 97-round mag. drums)
Turret Demon	Kestrel V-DR 696hp	202 mph – 15,000ft	28,800ft (8778m)	37ft 3in (11.35m)	29ft 7in (8.993m)	As Demon I. (Lewis gun mounted in FN turret)
Gauntlet I and II	Bristol Mercury VIS2 radial 640hp	231 mph – 15,800ft	33,500ft (10210m)	32ft 9½in (9.982m)	26ft 5in (8.077m)	2x .303 Vickers Mk.V (600 rpg)
Gladiator I	Bristol Mercury IX radial 830hp	253 mph – 14,500ft	32,800ft (9997m)	32ft 3in (9.829m)	27ft 5in (8.382m)	4x .303 Browning. (two in fuselage with 600rpg: two in wings with 400 rpg
Gladiator II	Bristol Mercury VIIIAS radial 830hp	257 mph – 14,600ft	33,500ft (10210m)	32ft 3in (9.829m)	27ft 5in (8.382m)	As per Mk.I
Hurricane I DH two-pitch prop (1939)	R-R Merlin II or III in-line 1030hp	315 mph – 17,500ft	33,200ft (10119m)	40ft 0in (12.19m)	31ft 5in (9.60m)	8x .303 Browning. (2,660 rounds in total)
Spitfire I DH two-pitch prop (1939)	Merlin III, 1030hp (fitted from 175th airframe onward)	357 mph – 18,600ft	34,400ft (10485m)	36ft 10in (11.21m)	29ft 11in (9.128m)	8x .303 Browning mg. (2,400 rounds)
Blenheim If	2 x Bristol Mercury VIII radials, 840hp each	c.263 mph – 10,000ft	31,400ft (9571m)	56ft 4in (17.17m)	39ft 9in (12.11)	1x .303 Browning in port wing 4x .303 Browning in ventral tray (500 rpg) 1x Vickers 'K' .303 in dorsal turret
Blenheim IVf	2 x Bristol Mercury XV radials, 920hp each	c.265 mph – 11,700ft	27,260 ft (8,309 m)	56ft 4in (17.17m)	42ft 7in (13.01m)	
Defiant I	Merlin III, 1030hp	304 mph – 17,000ft 250 mph – sea level	28,100ft (8,564m)	39ft 4in (11.98m)	35ft 4in (10.77m)	4x .303 Brownings in power-operated turret

*Specific engine data is nominal, fluctuating according to the source consulted – a consequence of the fact that power output varied with altitude, attitude, whether an engine was naturally aspirated or supercharged, and the demands made by the pilot. For comprehensive data covering specific engines please refer to 'British Piston Aero-Engines' by Alec Lumsden (Airlife).

Appendix 3: RAF fighter colour schemes 1920 to 1939 explained

By the end of World War One, the standard colour scheme for day fighters (and day bombers) serving on the Western Front in the newly named Royal Air Force, (formed on 1 April 1918 by amalgamating the Royal Flying Corps and the Royal Naval Air Service), was a cellulose-based dope called **PC10**, (Protective Colouring No 10), a greeny/brown/khaki shade made up from pigments of yellow ochre, umber, red ochre and Chinese blue. Applied to the upper surfaces of the mainplane, tailplane, fuselage top and sides and often the fin, it met the three-fold need of stretching and tautening the linen fabric over the framework which helped to strengthen the structure, reduce drag and improve the integrity of the covering as well as protecting it from the harmful rays of the sun and aided in the concealment of the aircraft when dispersed on the ground.

To apply it to Irish Linen fabric, a cellulose or oil varnish mixture was added, which caused an optical effect known as 'green shift', making the doped area look greenish under some light conditions depending on the type of varnish used. To add to the colour confusion, the colouring could also vary between manufacturers, and even from batch to batch by the same manufacturer, plus, as the aeroplane was exposed to the elements and the effects of fading, the green shift was reduced and it took on a browner appearance. Aeroplanes destined for service in hotter climes were doped with **PC12**, containing more red oxide and was more resistant to the penetration of the sun's rays, which created a distinctive reddish-brown colour.

The undersides were, naturally, not subject to as much exposure to sunlight as the upper surfaces, so the under surfaces of the mainplane, tailplanes and fuselage were invariably doped with a transparent covering, **V114**, that left them in their natural 'light creamy fawn' colour, often referred to as Clear Doped Linen.

By 1918, national markings (originally introduced in 1915) had standardised on a roundel design, similar to the ones applied to French aircraft but with the order of the colours reversed, comprising a red centre surrounded by a white ring surrounded by a blue outer ring, generally to a 1-3-5 ratio of proportionally spaced ring widths. When displayed on the PC10/PC12 upper surfaces, it was usual to outline the roundel with a white 1 inch wide surround. Also introduced in 1915 was rudder striping, in red, white and blue, with the blue forward, nearest the rudder post. Aircraft serial numbers were usually applied on the rear fuselage sides or, on some designs, the fin strake in black 8 inch high characters on the early clear-doped linen airframes, or across the rudder stripes on aircraft types without fuselages, such as the DH2 and FE2b, but on the PC10/PC12 camouflaged surfaces they didn't show up, so while some manufacturers persisted in painting the serials in black, others outlined them in white, with Sopwith applying them within a white rectangular box on the rear fuselage. The serials were invariably repeated across the rudder stripes, again outlined in white across the red and blue stripes.

Unit markings (generally geometric symbols) and individual aircraft markings (letters or numbers) on PC10 and PC12 doped aircraft were usually applied in white, the best colour to make them visible, generally on the fuselage sides and often on the top mainplane and under the lower mainplane.

Silver wings

After the end of WWI, the need to camouflage RAF aircraft that were dispersed on the ground diminished, and in the early 1920s, a superior, anti-ultraviolet light, finish was introduced by adding aluminium powder into the cellulose-based dope to create the **V84** Aluminium scheme that was gradually introduced on new aircraft designs, or when older WWI vintage aircraft were re-doped.

Roundels were retained as national markings and applied to the upper surfaces of the top mainplane, under surfaces of the lower mainplane and the fuselage sides in **VR3** Bright Red, **VW3** White and **VB2** Bright Blue, again, usually to a 1-3-5 ratio, although Armstrong Whitworth opted for a 1-2-3 ratio of equally spaced ring widths. The diameter of the fuselage roundels appears to have been 25 inches on all the aircraft types, but both the upper and lower mainplane roundels varied in diameter, essentially spanning the chord from leading to trailing edge, so were determined by the aircraft's design. Rudder stripes were also retained, in red, white and blue, still with blue nearest the rudder post.

Serial numbers continued to be applied on the rear fuselage sides and on the rudder, in black characters, ranging from 6 inches to 9 inches high, with those on the rudder being outlined in white on the red and blue stripes. The aircraft manufacturers applied serial numbers on the production line, in their own individual styles, there being no standard font or style for them. In an attempt to discourage unnecessary low-flying and show-off manoeuvres, in March 1927, serial numbers were ordered to be applied to the underside of the lower mainplane, reading from the front (leading edge) under the port wing and from the rear (trailing edge) under the starboard wing. Again, the height of their application was determined by the chord of the wing and/or the position and diameter of the underwing roundels.

Introduction of squadron markings

Despite there being relatively few aircraft in RAF service, as early as mid-1922, the few home-based fighter squadrons that were left, started applying individual unit markings to their Aluminium-doped aircraft. Primarily the result of individual initiative within the squadrons, the practice of applying unit markings along the fuselage sides in the form of coloured bars, checks or zig-zags, soon came to the attention of higher command and, perhaps surprisingly, received favourable approval, resulting in an Air Ministry Order, dated December 1924, giving official authority for the practice to continue, together with applying Flight colours to mainwheel discs and/or fins – red for A Flight, yellow for B Flight, and blue for C Flight.

It was recognised that the application of squadron colours encouraged *esprit de corps* and a healthy rivalry between the squadrons leading to enhanced operational efficiency. The practice continued to flourish and by 1930 all RAF fighter squadrons had developed and applied unique squadron markings that were also applied to the upper surfaces of the upper mainplane.

Appendix 3: RAF: RAF fighter colour schemes 1920 to 1939 explained
Continued

Rudder stripes and roundel changes

In August 1930, an Air Ministry Order (AMO) was sent out to all RAF squadrons to reverse the colour sequence of the rudder stripes with red nearest the rudder post. Primarily this was to differentiate them from the French practice and squadrons were officially given until October 1930 to facilitate the change. Serial numbers were retained across the rudder stripes, again outlined in white across the red and blue stripes.

Later, in August 1934, an AMO was issued requiring all upper and lower (if applicable) mainplane roundels to be reduced in diameter so that they did not overlap the ailerons. The 1-2-3 Red/White/Blue ratio was retained. At the same time, it was ordered that rudder striping was to be discontinued – both being the result of concerns about the over-balancing of control surfaces. Serial numbers were retained on the rudder, in the traditional letter above the numeral's application.

Squadron badges

During the early 1930s, squadrons began applying their own informal badges and insignia (many dating from WWI) to the fins of their aircraft. However, a process of formalising squadron badges was started and in March 1935, the then Chester Herald of Arms in Ordinary, Mr J D Heaton-Armstrong, was appointed the first Inspector of RAF Badges. His role was to advise the Air Ministry on heraldic matters, and the first thing he did was to produce a Standard Frame to encircle all badges to ensure uniformity. The badges were 'ensigned' on the top with a King's Crown, (the ruling monarch at the time being Edward VIII*)

In January 1936, an Air Ministry Order (A.8/1936) was issued detailing the criteria for badges and their ultimate approval via the Chester Herald and the reigning monarch. The first badges were approved by Edward VIII in May 1936, to numbers 2, 4, 15, 18, 19, 22, 33, 201, 207, 216 and 604 Squadrons, of which only 19 Squadron was equipped with fighters. The whole design process would ultimately rest with the Chester Herald as the Inspector of RAF Badges, who would liaise with squadrons and units to finalise designs that reflected already adopted insignia or to utilise something suitable to recognise the squadron or unit.

Simplified images, referred to as motifs, were regularly extracted from squadron badges and applied to the fin, often within another design that was introduced in 1936, under AMO A14/36, which identified the role of the squadron or unit – be it fighter (in the form of a spearhead), bomber (a spherical grenade) or a star for reconnaissance/army co-operation units.

*The number of badges approved by Edward VIII were small in number; the period between his accession to the throne and his abdication lasted only eleven months. As the first batch of badges for the approval process was completed in July 1936, most badges were approved by his successor, King George VI, and later by HM Queen Elizabeth II, those badges being 'ensigned' on the top with a Queen's Crown.

Creation of Fighter Command

Prior to the creation of the Command structure, the RAF had been split into Areas – home-based fighters being established as Fighting Area, (bombers as Bomber Area and maritime reconnaissance aircraft as Coastal Area). In June 1926, the Fighting Area was changed to Air Defence of Great Britain (ADGB). In an attempt to achieve parity with Nazi Germany's perceived increasing air strength, a number of schemes were introduced for the rapid expansion of the RAF, including a major change in the command structure.

On 1 May 1936, the Area formations were restructured into command status and were now to be called Commands. Air Defence of Great Britain was renamed Fighter Command, Bomber Area became Bomber Command, and Coastal Area became Coastal Command. Although the restructuring didn't directly affect any changes to markings , a research programme started in 1933, carried out under the supervision of the Chemistry Department of the Royal Aircraft Establishment (RAE) at Farnborough, had been looking into the camouflaging of RAF aircraft again.

Re-introduction of camouflage

On 14 February 1933, the Air Ministry asked the RAE to investigate means of reducing the visibility of an aircraft when viewed from above, when on the ground, or in flight. The results of the experiment were submitted to the Air Ministry during the following August in an RAE report entitled 'Note on Colour Schemes to Decrease Visibility of Aircraft from Above.' Some work had already been done on aircraft camouflage at Orfordness during WWI, which led to the conclusion that broad, irregular curves or stripes of contrasting colours, in appropriate shades to match the background, should run diagonally across the aircraft and be carried as far as possible over the engine cowling, fuselage and tail without stopping at any important structural point.

The most suitable colours seemed self-evident as against the average European background, various shades of green and brown would suffice. A range of colours, from a dark green to a light sand were compared with various backgrounds such as trees, grass, heather, and sand. From these samples a number of colours were selected which harmonised with the backgrounds. Only a few of these colours were then chosen for the next stage of the experiment, which was to find the most suitable sizes of the different coloured patches.

Little consideration seems to have been given to the matter of the identification markings because the report makes no mention of them, but it seems that they were all removed from the upper surfaces with the exception of one of the upper wing roundels, and this was modified in the dull red and blue shades used on night flying aircraft. The final point was that to avoid bright reflections from the aircraft, matt colours were desirable, with both nitrocellulose dopes and distemper materials and colours being tested. Flight tests were carried out using a Fairey Gordon to refine the scheme, and on 21 July 1933, it was flown in company with three other machines which were finished in **NIVO** (an acronym for Night Invisible Varnish Orfordness), PC10, and V84 Aluminium for comparisons to be made.

Over a whole range of backgrounds, the camouflaged Gordon was more difficult to see. The combination of greens and browns admirably suited the trees, cornfields and dried-up vegetation of the summer months and the report concluded that a number of machines operating in various parts of the country should be painted in the same scheme as that worn by the Gordon and observations made as to the value of the scheme in comparison with NIVO which had been judged the second best camouflage scheme after the new RAE scheme.

The Air Ministry was sufficiently impressed to order service trials of the new scheme in January 1934. These evidently took some time to arrange because it was not until mid-June that 4 and 111 Squadrons (equipped with Hawker Audax and Bristol Bulldogs respectively) received supplies of four colours called **Dark Earth**, **Dark Green**, **Light Earth** and **Light Green** to enable the service trials to commence. Like the trials at the RAE, the service trials were considered to be successful with the camouflaged aircraft showing a marked superiority over the standard NIVO and Aluminium schemes. As a result, at the end of December 1934, the Air Ministry ordered further trials of the scheme in the Middle East and ordered work to start on developing a similar sort of camouflage for a sea scheme.

Abyssinian Crisis
It was at this time that the Abyssinian Crisis erupted. On 6 December 1934, Emperor Haile Selassie of Ethiopia protested to the League of Nations about Italian incursions and aggression in the Walwal area of Ethiopia, then commonly known as Abyssinia. Although the League of Nations ruled against Italy and voted for economic sanctions, they were never fully applied and Italy quit the League. Italian armed forces eventually invaded Ethiopia without a declaration of war on 3 October 1935, thus began the Second Italo-Ethiopian War to create what became known as the Abyssinian Crisis.

As a result of Italian aggression in Abyssinia, there was a sudden need for some kind of camouflage for those aircraft sent to Malta to strengthen Britain's presence in the Mediterranean should the crisis lead to war with Italy. Quantities of camouflage paint developed by the RAE in both land and sea camouflage colours were despatched to Malta, and the aircraft of 22 and 202 (bomber) Squadrons, and 74 (fighter) Squadron which had just re-formed. Equipped with Hawker Demons, 74 Squadron was based at Hal Far, and all their aircraft received camouflage finishes of one sort or another. The paint was applied by the units themselves over the existing Aluminium dope finish to various prescribed camouflage patterns.

From the available black and white photos, it is difficult to accurately determine what each particular aircraft's colour scheme actually was, but Dark Earth, Dark Green, Light Earth and Light Green and a grey colour, possibly Dark Sea Grey, were amongst the RAE paint samples sent to Malta for use on the 'Land Plane Scheme'. To further confuse matters, at least two of the RAE colours were 'modified' – one by adding red dope to Dark Earth to make a dark red-brown colloquially called 'Malta Soil', and white dope to Light Earth to make a beige shade referred to as 'Malta Rock'. Under surfaces appear to have been kept in the original V84 Aluminium finish with the original 1-3-5 ratio VR3 Bright Red, VW3 White and VB2 Bright Blue roundels and black serial numbers retained under the wings. All other national markings appear to have been overpainted, with just a single red/blue roundel, applied in the dull **VNR5** and **VNB6** shades, in varying positions on the upper mainplane of different aircraft.

The Temperate Land Scheme
With the first operational use of camouflage on Malta being judged a success, the question of whether to adopt camouflage for the whole of the RAF arose. The issue was debated at a conference held at the Air Ministry on 13 February 1936, to determine the policy with regard to the camouflaging of aircraft, chaired by the Air Member for Research and Development, Air Marshal Sir Hugh C T Dowding, (Air Chief Marshal from 1 January 1937), who became the first C-in-C of the newly created RAF Fighter Command in July 1936, and was later to gain immortal fame as the C-in-C of Fighter Command during the Battle of Britain.

The general conclusion reached was that camouflage should be adopted, but only for home-based aircraft. Of these, fighters and light bombers would only be camouflaged in Dark Earth and Dark Green on the upper surfaces, with the under surfaces remaining in Aluminium, whilst medium and heavy bombers were to be camouflaged Dark Earth/Dark Green on the upper surfaces, and a plain dark blue-black mixture called **Night**, that produced a finish which offered not only low reflectivity but a degree of durability on the under surfaces. (see 'Before the Storm Vol 2: RAF Bomber 1930–1939'). The new Night shade would also be convenient for serial number and identification lettering on camouflaged surfaces and as an overall finish on propeller blades.

Once the decision to introduce camouflage had been taken, standards for the new colours were passed out to paint manufacturers and new material specifications were drawn up for both cellulose and synthetic based paints that would be suitable for finishing the new metal monoplanes which would shortly be entering service as part of the expansion of the RAF.

Air Diagrams
At the end of February 1936, the RAE was instructed to draw up camouflage scheme patterns for the Fairey Battle, Bristol Blenheim, Armstrong Whitworth Whitley, Handley Page Hampden and Vickers Wellesley. However, the Directorate of Technical Development suggested that it would be expedient if instead of preparing an individual design for each aircraft type, a generic scheme could be drawn up for a typical single-engined monoplane and a typical twin-engined monoplane.

As a result of the work on aircraft camouflage undertaken up until this point, the first three camouflage scheme drawings, which were prepared in June 1936, showed three colours – Dark Green, Dark Earth and Night, on three Air Diagrams, AD 1157 'Camouflage Scheme for Twin Engine Monoplanes - Heavy Bombers'; AD 1158, 'Camouflage Scheme for Single Engine Monoplanes - Medium bombers'; and AD 1159, 'Camouflage Scheme for Twin Engine Monoplanes - Medium Bombers'. These schemes were applied to the Handley Page Harrow, Fairey Battle and Bristol Blenheim respectively. The next Air Diagram to be drawn up, AD 1160, started life as the 'Camouflage Scheme for Single Engine Monoplanes - Army Co-operation', intended for use on the Westland Lysander, in October 1936. However, work was proceeding apace on the new monoplane fighters and by November 1936, work on the Hawker Hurricane had progressed far enough for representatives of the RAE to visit Hawkers to discuss the camouflage scheme which was to be applied to production aircraft. This was then followed by a similar visit to Supermarine in February 1937. These visits cumulated in the RAE submitting a drawing to the Air Ministry on 9 March 1937, entitled 'Camouflage Scheme for High Speed Interceptor Monoplanes'. It was suggested that this scheme would also be suitable for the Westland Lysander, so once the Air Ministry had approved the design, it was tidied up, and re-submitted on 25 March 1937 as Air Diagram 1160, 'Camouflage Scheme for Single Engine Monoplanes'.

A and B Schemes
The Air Diagram camouflage patterns were further broken down into A Scheme and B Scheme, essentially mirror images of each other that were to be applied on alternating airframes on the production line. The demarcation line between the Dark Earth/Dark Green Temperate Land Scheme on the upper surfaces and the under surfaces, which initially remained in Aluminium on fighters, army co-operation types and light bombers, followed a line at a tangent of 60 degrees to the horizontal, low down on the fuselage side, known

Appendix 3: RAF: RAF fighter colour schemes 1920 to 1939 explained
Continued

as Pattern No 1. (NB: There is reason to believe that the RAE actually produced four scheme designations – the 'A' and 'B' Schemes, and 'C' and 'D' Schemes. These would most likely have been identical to the 'A' and 'B' Schemes, but with the positions of the Dark Earth and Dark Green areas transposed. At least one Fairey Battle is known to have flown operationally during the Battle of France in one of these transposed schemes, but whether any other aircraft types were so finished is unknown.)

Munich Crisis: changes
While plans were being made to camouflage all new and forthcoming aircraft types, Hitler's territorial ambitions (discussed elsewhere in this volume) threatened to propel Europe into another World War, most particularly as a consequence of the September 1938 Munich crisis.

Originally, the Air Ministry had no intention of camouflaging the RAF's existing biplanes then in service as they were due to be gradually replaced by modern monoplanes; but the Munich Crisis and a very real threat of war, forced a decision to camouflage *all* home-based frontline aircraft including Fighter Command's Furies, Demons, Gauntlets and Gladiators. At a stroke, the squadron's colourful identification markings were gone, painted over with drab camouflage. At this time no Air Diagram camouflage patterns had been designed for biplanes, so all the aircraft were painted in Dark Earth and Dark Green upper surfaces to whatever patterns were deemed suitable, many being based upon simplified versions of the new Air Diagrams for single engined monoplanes such as AD 1158 and AD 1160.

Several other changes were made during this period following the camouflaging of existing aircraft including a general toning down of the roundels. Those on the wing upper surfaces and fuselage sides were modified or overpainted into low-visibility red and blue roundels, invariably applied in dull VNR5 and VNB6 shades. The only marking that appears to have survived the toning-down exercise on Fighter Command's aircraft was the 'spearhead' on the fin, but not all squadrons kept even that.

Night and White undersides for fighters
Although it had been decided that home-based fighters (and light bombers) would only be camouflaged on the upper surfaces, with the under surfaces remaining in Aluminium, the introduction of Chain Home, the codename for the ring of coastal Radio Direction Finding (RDF) early warning stations, developed by Sir Robert Watson-Watt's research station at Bawdsey Manor, created an aircraft identification problem. The successful demonstration of RDF, (later know as RADAR, an acronym coined in 1940 by the US Navy for Radio Detection and Ranging), in February 1935 resulted in immediate funding for a chain of RDF stations around the east coast of the British Isles from Orkney in the north to Weymouth in the south, and by 1936 the first five stations had been commissioned in the south-east of England to protect the Thames Estuary and London.

However, one of the problems encountered in building the world's first integrated air defence system lay in finding some means of identifying friendly fighter aircraft once they had passed inland and beyond RDF's ability to continue tracking them. (Early RDF systems transmitted signals through 360 degrees, consequently, in order for operators to tell from which direction a return was coming, the inland 180 degree segment had to be blocked out electronically.) Thereafter, in order to avoid being shot at by anti-aircraft gunners, Home Defence fighters had to be identified, tracked, and plotted visually from the ground as they crossed the coast and headed inland.

In recognition of this, an Air Ministry decision was made on 30 August 1938, that Home Defence fighter aircraft were to have the undersides of their wings and tailplanes painted in Night and White, following previous field trials held in early 1938, to allow the Royal Observer Corps (ROC) to track them. It was decided that the under surface of the port wing was to be finished in Night, and the under surface of the starboard wing in White, with the flaps and ailerons included in this colour scheme – the division between the colours running down the centreline of the aircraft. Serial numbers under the starboard wing of the aircraft were to remain in Night as they were at present, but those under the port wing were to be applied in White so as to be visible, although this order was soon amended and underwing serial numbers were painted over on all types except training aircraft. The Air Ministry also concluded that there was no legal reason why national markings (roundels) on the underside of Home Defence fighter aircraft were necessary, as the Night and White finish would act as sufficient identification from below and the roundels only served to break up the clean expanse of Night and White which was being relied upon for recognition, so on 30 August 1938, the Director of Operations and Intelligence wrote to Fighter Command to inform them of the decisions.

From 23 September 1938, the Night and White under surface scheme spread very quickly amongst the Home Defence squadrons, with the biplane aircraft already in service with Aluminium under surfaces being repainted by the squadrons or maintenance units (MUs). The wings of these aircraft, (but not their ailerons), were to be repainted in squadron service as it appears to have been decided that as the Aluminium ailerons did not appear to detract greatly from the Night and White scheme, their continued use would be accepted for the time being. However, arrangements were to be made to paint spare ailerons held in store in the correct Night or White colours so that they would gradually replace the incorrectly finished ones in units. Ultimately it was decided that the painting of the under surfaces of the ailerons would be undertaken by the manufacturers at their service depots.

It was almost inevitable that this would throw up some anomalies, which included examples with just the underside of the lower mainplane being painted Night and White (the underside of the upper mainplane remaining in Aluminium); the underside of the nose, the rear fuselage aft of the wing trailing edge, and sometimes the tailplanes and elevators remaining in Aluminium; or bizarrely, ailerons being painted in the opposite colour to the rest of the wing (i.e. Night on White and White on Night)! Another anomaly, illustrated by one of the photos in this book, was Night and White being applied under the wrong side, with White appearing under the port undersides and Night under the starboard undersides.

There was some delay before new aircraft began to leave the production line in this new under surface scheme, and again misinterpretation of the instructions, with early delivery Hurricanes only having the outer (fabric) wing panels in the Night and White scheme, or just the mainplane in Night and White with the underside of the nose, the rear fuselage aft of the wing trailing edge, and the tailplanes and elevators in Aluminium. At Supermarine for example, it was not until April 1939 before Spitfires began to leave the production line with Night/White under surfaces, previous deliveries often displaying similar anomalies to the Hurricanes.

An exception to the Night/White rule was made for fighter aircraft stationed in France, in AMO A.520 dated 7 December 1939, which stated that Fighter aircraft stationed in France were to carry Red, White and Blue roundels under the wings.

Introduction of code letters

During the Munich Crisis, it was decided to adopt a standard system of identification markings on aircraft of operational squadrons throughout the whole of the RAF, both at home and overseas, consisting of code letters to identify squadrons and individual aircraft within a squadron. Comprising of two letters to identify the squadron, they were to be placed either forward or aft of the fuselage roundel, with a single letter, to indicate the individual aircraft within the squadron, placed on the other side of the fuselage roundel. These code letters were to be applied at squadron level, using **Medium Sea Grey** paint and to be 48 inches high with 6 inch wide strokes, with letters smaller than this only being used when lack of space made the use of the specified dimensions impossible – e.g., on most of the 'smaller' fighter aircraft such as the Gauntlets and Gladiators. There was no set style for these markings and considerable variation could be seen in how they were actually applied to the aircraft, as well as in the exact shade of grey paint used to apply them.

Upon the outbreak of World War Two, all RAF squadrons had their two letter squadron code allocation changed as a security measure to confuse the enemy… *or almost all*. Some took longer than others to change: 616 Squadron for instance retained its code 'QJ' from October 1939 until October 1941.

Serial numbers

Serial numbers continued to be applied by the manufacturer on the production line, in Night, and were to be 8 inches high, with individual characters not more than 5 inches wide and made up of brush strokes of 1 inch in width. They were to be applied to the rear fuselage and the rudder, although by early 1939, those on the rudder were beginning to be removed (or overpainted), and on many aircraft the fuselage serial number was also overpainted too. As mentioned previously, underwing serial numbers were invariably overpainted or removed, although a few examples on early production Hurricanes and some Blenheims would be seen for a few more months. As there was no standard font or style for serial numbers, aircraft manufacturers continued to apply them in their own individual styles.

Shadow Compensating Scheme

With war becoming increasingly inevitable, a Temperate Land Scheme camouflage for biplanes, was devised in April 1939 – AD1162 for Single Engine Biplanes, Army Co-operation Aeroplanes and Fighters – which comprised four colours: Dark Earth and Dark Green (for the upper surfaces of the top mainplane, upper half of the fuselage and cowling, the fin and rudder, and tailplane; and Light Earth and Light Green for the upper surfaces of the lower mainplane and lower parts of fuselage and cowling. This scheme became known as the Shadow Compensating Scheme, and the AD drawings were based upon the Gladiator, which was the only biplane fighter type still in limited production at the time. AD1162 had an A and B Scheme application, essentially mirror images of each other, that were to be applied on alternating airframes on the production line.

Hurricanes and Spitfires

In June 1936, the Hawker Hurricane, the first of the eight-gun monoplane fighters, was formally ordered into production, the Air Ministry having placed its first order that month for 600 aircraft. In December 1937, the first four Hurricanes to enter RAF service joined 111 Squadron, stationed at RAF Northolt, and by the following February had received sixteen Hurricanes.

Camouflaged on the production line, in Dark Earth and Dark Green upper surfaces from the outset, in the mirror image A and B Schemes on alternating airframes on the production line, the under surfaces preceded the introduction of the Night/White scheme and were painted Aluminium to Pattern No 1. To make the roundels sufficiently visible in peacetime, the Red, White and Blue 1-3-5 ratio roundels were outlined in Yellow on the upper surfaces of the wings and the fuselage sides, in a 1-3-5-7 ratio. Upper wing roundels were 49 inch diameter and those on the fuselage sides, 35 inch diameter. Underwing roundels were 45 inches in diameter. Despite being officially standardised at 8 inches, the height of the fuselage serial numbers on the initial batches of Hurricanes, was 6 inches, but later batches had corrected 8 inch serials. Serial numbers under the wings, were 30 inches in height, reading from the front under the port wing and from the rear under the starboard wing. All serial numbers were applied in Night.

As mentioned above, due to some rather ambiguous wording in the official directive regarding the application of the Night/White under surfaces, the first deliveries following the type's introduction, (L1576 to L1625), saw the Night and White only being applied to the fabric covered wing sections outboard of the main (metal) centre section, the rest of the under surfaces remaining in Aluminium. The serial numbers under the port (Night) wings were painted in White, while the numbers under the starboard wings remained in Night. Forty-five inch diameter Red/White/Blue roundels were also applied under the wings. These errors were partially corrected in subsequent deliveries, but still not quite how Dowding or the Air Ministry had intended, but at least the Night/White under surfaces now met along the aircraft's centreline, but only from the leading to the trailing edge of the wing, with the nose, rear fuselage and tailplanes still being in Aluminium. In this version, the underwing roundels hadn't been applied, although the serial numbers were still in evidence! Finally, Hawkers got it right and the main production batches that followed had just the Night/White scheme covering the entire under surfaces, (no roundels or serial numbers), with the division of the two colours running down the aircraft's centreline, including the nose, fuselage and tailplane undersides. Aircraft that had already been delivered and were in squadron service or at MUs, underwent similar inconsistencies with ailerons either left in Aluminium or painted in opposing Night/White colours to the rest of the wing surfaces, and with the nose, rear fuselage and tailplanes remaining in Aluminium. Roundels on the wing upper surfaces and fuselage sides were also modified into the low visibility red and blue style, invariably in the dull matt VNR5 and VNB6 shades, generally by using the outer edge of the Blue ring as the outer diameter, (vthe Yellow ring being completely overpainted in the surrounding camouflage colours), and extending the Red and Blue over the White, resulting in the fuselage roundels being 25 inches diameter and the upper wing roundels 35 inches in diameter.

When first in service, 111 Squadron's Hurricanes had the squadron's number '111' applied to the fuselage, aft of the roundel, for a short time, in white, for the Squadron's commander, and the top third of the numbers additionally painted in the Flight colours of red and blue for the rest of the aircraft.

Appendix 3: RAF: RAF fighter colour schemes 1920 to 1939 explained
Continued

Having a slightly deeper fuselage side than many of the previous generation of biplanes, and indeed the forthcoming Spitfire, Hurricanes could accommodate slightly larger code letters when they were introduced in the summer of 1938, but even so, 36 to 40 inch high letters tended to be the largest applied. The only pre-camouflage period markings that appear to have been carried by Hurricanes were small squadron badges within a standard frame or the fighter 'spearhead', both of which were applied on the fin, but neither remained for long as the threat of war became more apparent and were painted over by the outbreak of war in September 1939.

Spitfires also went through similar colour scheme markings changes. The Air Ministry placed an order for 310 Spitfires (also) in June 1936, with production beginning at Supermarine's factory at Woolston. However, Supermarine was a small company, already busy building Walrus and Stranraer flying boats, and Vickers was busy building Wellington bombers, so it soon became apparent that the order clearly could not be completed within the fifteen months promised. Despite this, the managements of Supermarine and Vickers were able to convince the Air Ministry that production problems could be overcome, and further orders were placed.

Again, camouflaged on the production line in Dark Earth and Dark Green upper surfaces, in A and B Schemes on alternating airframes, with under surfaces painted Aluminium, to Pattern No 1, the first production Spitfires came off the assembly line in May 1938, almost twenty-four months after the initial order was placed; the first Mk.I, K9789, entering service with 19 Squadron at RAF Duxford on 4 August 1938. Immediately pre-dating the Munich Crisis colour scheme and marking changes, 19 Squadron's first Spitfires had the full Red/White/Blue/Yellow roundels on the upper surfaces of the wings and the fuselage sides, in a 1-3-5-7 ratio. Upper wing roundels were 56 inch diameter and those on the fuselage sides, 35 inch diameter. Underwing roundels were 50 inches in diameter. Night, 8 inch high, serial numbers were applied to the rear fuselage and under the wings, 12 inches in height, due to the lack of space between the roundel and the mainwheel well, reading from the front under the port wing and from the rear under the starboard wing.

For a noticeably short period, (perhaps only a few days), the unit's Spitfires carried the number '19' on the fin in what appears to have been White, although at least one, K9797, had a Red '19' which may have been the squadron leader's aircraft. However, with the introduction of code letters and requirement for low visibility red and blue roundels due to the Munich Crisis, the aircraft soon took on a more sombre look. Again, by using the outer edge of the Blue ring as the outer diameter, (the Yellow ring being completely overpainted in the surrounding camouflage colours), and extending the red and blue over the White, it resulted in the fuselage roundels being 25 inches diameter and the upper wing roundels 40 inches in diameter.

The application of Night/White under surfaces went through similar anomalous variations to all the other Fighter Command aircraft, with the Night/White meeting along the aircraft's centreline but only from the leading to the trailing edge of the wing, with the nose, rear fuselage and tailplanes still being in Aluminium; ailerons either being left in Aluminium or painted in opposing Night/White colours to the rest of the wing surfaces; and roundels and/or serial numbers being left in situ, before the official standard Night/White division running down the aircraft's centreline, including the nose, fuselage and tailplane undersides, without roundels or serial numbers, was achieved. The Spitfire's slim fuselage meant that when code letters were introduced in the summer of 1938, they were generally applied using 24 to 30 inch high characters in Medium Sea Grey. The only pre-camouflage period markings that appear to have been carried by Spitfires was the fighter spearhead on the fin, seen on some 54 and 72 Squadron machines, but by the outbreak of war they too were overpainted.

Blenheim fighters
Designed as a bomber, no Blenheim fighters were built as such, but some 200 Mk.I airframes were converted (mainly by MUs from airframes held in storage), by adding an underfuselage gun pack housing four .303in Browning machine guns and re-designated Mk.If. The first Blenheim If fighters were allocated to 600 (Auxiliary Air Force) Squadron based at Hendon, in September 1938, replacing the unit's Hawker Demons. Other ex-Demon squadrons, including 23, 25, 29, and 604, were re-equipped with the twin-engined Mk.If during the winter of 1938, with at least seven Fighter Command squadrons becoming operational on the type by early 1939.

Like the Hurricane and Spitfire, the Blenheim was camouflaged in Dark Earth and Dark Green upper surfaces from the outset, in alternating A and B Schemes, but in this instance to Air Diagram AD 1159 'Camouflage Scheme for Twin Engine Monoplanes - Medium Bombers' and, being a bomber, had Night under surfaces which made the application of the Night/White fighter under surfaces a little easier, albeit not without its almost inevitable anomalies! Initially, a common expedient was to simply overpaint the starboard wing and starboard tailplane in White, often leaving the whole of the fuselage underside, the starboard aileron and the starboard elevator in the original Night. Even when the correct Night/White division down the fuselage centreline had been achieved, the underside of the starboard engine cowling was often left in the original Night, and occasionally the starboard aileron and the starboard elevator too.

Serial numbers were applied in Night, 8 inch high characters on the rear fuselage and on the rudder, and 36 inches high under the wings, in White on the Night under surfaces. As such, underwing serials were occasionally left under the port wing in White, (the one under the starboard wing being overpainted with the application of the White).

The original roundels were modified in the same way as all the other types, by using the outer edge of the Blue ring as the outer diameter, (the Yellow ring being completely overpainted in the surrounding camouflage colours), and extending the red and blue over the White, which in the Blenheim's case resulted in the fuselage roundels being 32½ inches diameter and the upper wing roundels 47½ inches in diameter. Occasionally Red/Blue roundels were applied under one or both wings, but this was the exception rather than the rule.

However, the factory-applied position of the fuselage roundel and the large wing/fuselage fillet fairing at the trailing edge of the Blenheim's wings created problems in the positioning of the code letters. It became common practice on Fighter Command aircraft for the two-letter squadron code to be placed to left of the fuselage roundel and the individual aircraft letter to the right of the fuselage roundel, which on the port side of the Blenheim's fuselage meant there was little room between the fuselage roundel and the large wing/fuselage fillet fairing. Some squadrons (e.g., 248 Squadron) physically moved the port fuselage roundel by overpainting the original and painting a new one further aft along the fuselage, but most either extended the code letters over the wing/fuselage fillet fairing or simply applied the squadron codes to the right of the fuselage roundel on the port side and applied the single individual aircraft letter to the left of the roundel.

Glossary and Abbreviations

AACU	Anti-Aircraft Cooperation Unit
AAF	Auxiliary Air Force'
AEE	Aeroplane Experimental Establishment
A&AEE	Aeroplane & Armament Experimental Establishment
A&GS	Armament and Gunnery School
AAS	Air Armament School
AMO	Air Ministry Order
AOS	Air Observers School
ASU	aircraft storage unit
ATS	Advanced Training Squadrons
auw	all-up weight
B&GS	Bombing & Gunnery School
BEF	British Expeditionary Force (1939)
CFS	Central Flying School
CO	Commanding Officer
CSU	constant speed unit
DBR	damaged beyond repair
FAA	Fleet Air Arm
FBTS	Flying Boat Training Squadron
FTS	Flying Training School
GDGS	Ground Defence Gunners School
GP	General-Purpose (aircraft)
HAD	Home Aircraft Depot, Henlow
MAEE	Marine Aircraft Experimental Establishment
MoS	Ministry of Supply
MU	Maintenance Unit
OTU	Operational Training Unit
PR	photographic reconnaissance/photo recce
RAAF	Royal Australian Air Force
RAE	Royal Aircraft Establishment
RAF	Royal Air Force
RAFC	RAF College
RCAF	Royal Canadian Air Force
RFC	Royal Flying Corps (merged with Royal Navy's RNAS to form the RAF on 1.4.1918)
RHAF	Royal Hellenic Air Force
RNZAF	Royal New Zealand Air Force
rpg	rounds per gun
rpm	rounds-per-minute
RPM	revolutions-per-minute
RNAS	Royal Naval Air Service (merged with British Army's RFC to form the RAF on 1.4.1918)
SAAF	South African Air Force
SFTS	Service Flying Training School
SOC	struck off charge
SoTT	School of Technical Training
STS	Seaplane Training Squadron
WFU	Withdrawn from use

Glossary and Abbreviations *continued*

RANKS

Sgt	Sergeant
F/Sgt	Flight Sergeant
P/O	Pilot Officer
F/O	Flying Officer
F/L	Flight Lieutenant
S/Ldr	Squadron Leader
W/C	Wing Commander
G/C	Group Captain

Colour Clarity: the correct names for the colours used on RAF roundels.

Bright Red: pre-war colour used up to c.1937/38 referred to in MoS colour range as Aircraft Finish No.11A

Bright Blue: pre-war colour used up to c.1937/38 referred to in MoS colour range as Aircraft Finish No.12A

White: simply referred to as White in MoS colour range as Aircraft Finish No.1A **White**

Red: (or **Dull Red**) used from 1937/38. Simply referred to as Red until 1947 when it was replaced by **Post Office Red**

Blue: (or **Dull Blue**) used from 1937/38. Simply referred to as Blue until 1947 when it was replaced by **Roundel Blue**

Yellow: used 1937 to 1947, referred to in MoS colour range as Aircraft Finish No.2 and used to 1947 when replaced by **Golden Yellow**

Bibliography

Armament of British Aircraft 1909-1939: HF King; *Putnam & Co Ltd, 1971*

British Piston Aero Engines and Their Aircraft: Alec Lumsden; *Airlife Publishing Ltd, 1994*

British Fighter Since 1912, The: Francis K Mason; *Putnam Books, 1992*

British Aircraft At War 1935-45: Gordon Swanborough; *HPC Publishing, 1997*

Combat Codes -Since 1938: Vic Flintham and Andrew Thomas; *Airlife Publishing Ltd, 2003*

Fighter Squadrons of the RAF: John DR Rawlings; *Macdonald & Janes Ltd, 1978*

Flying Training and Support Units: R Sturtivant, J Hamlin; *Air-Britain (Historians) Ltd, 2007*

Flying Units of the RAF: A Lake; *Airlife Publishing Ltd, 1999*

Guns of the RAF 1939-1945: GF Wallace; *William Kimber and Co Ltd, 1972*

Hawker Hurricane, An Illustrated History, The: Francis K Mason; *Crecy, 1990*

Hawker Hurricane & Sea Hurricane, Flight Craft 3: Tony O'Toole; *Pen & Sword Books Ltd, 2014*

K File, The RAF of the 1930s, The: JJ Halley MBE; *Air-Britain (Historians) Ltd, 1995*

On Silver Wings, RAF Biplane Fighters Between the Wars: Alec Lumsden & Owen Thetford; *Osprey Aerospace, 1993*

Prelude To War – The RAF 1936-1939: Martin Derry; *Pen & Sword Books Ltd, 2020*

RAF Flying Training and Support Units since 1912: R Sturtivant & J Hamlin; *Air-Britain (Historians)Ltd, 2007*

Royal Air Force Aircraft serial monographs (various): *Air-Britain (Historians)Ltd*

RAF Squadrons: CG Jefford; *Airlife Publishing Ltd, 2001*

Squadrons of the Fleet Air Arm, The: Ray Sturtivant and Theo Ballance; *Air-Britain (Historians) Ltd, 1994*

Squadrons of the RAF and Commonwealth 1918-1988, The: JJ Halley; *Air-Britain (Historians) Ltd, 1988*

Warplanes of the Third Reich: William Green; *Macdonald & Jane's (Publishers) Limited, 1979*

Wings of Silver, The Silver Years of the RAF 1919-1939: Mike Starmer; *Aviation Workshop Publications Ltd, 2007*